The Guide to Tax Free Wealth 2019, 2020 & Beyond

Learn How the Wealthy Like Trump Use Cash Value Life Insurance, 1031 Real Estate Exchanges, 401k & IRA Investing, & Other Loopholes to Lower Taxes

By: Ryan Wright

TABLE OF CONTENTS

INTRODUCTION 1

BASIC OPTION 1: 401K or IRA? Why Not Both! 2

    401(k) 3

    IRA 9

BASIC OPTION 2: Investing in a Health Savings Account 16

    What is an HSA? 16

    How to Turn a HSA Into an Investment Vehicle 22

BASIC OPTION 3: Selling Your Home 25

    Know How to Choose the Right Time to Sell: 26

    Understand Your Market, the Economy, Your Neighborhood, Your Buyer 28

    How Much Will My Home Sale Cost? 29

    Adding Value Through Renovations 31

    Contact a Real Estate Agent: 35

    Set the Right Price and Negotiate the Best Offer 37

BASIC OPTION 4: Renting Your Home for 14 Days or Less 38

BASIC OPTION 5: Benefits of Investing in Municipal Bonds 43

    General obligation bonds: 46

    Revenue bonds: 47

    How do I invest in municipal bonds? 48

    How do I make money off of my municipal bonds? 49

COMPLEX OPTION 1: Cash Value Life Insurance Policies 52
    Whole Life Insurance 60
    Indexed Universal Life Insurance 63
COMPLEX OPTION 2: 1031 Exchanges 81
    What is a 1031 Exchange? 82
    What does "like-kind" mean? 85
    Four Types of 1031 Exchanges 91
COMPLEX OPTION 3: Investing in Qualified Opportunity Zones 96
    How Does This Investment Program Work? 99
Wrap Up: 105
BONUS: A Detailed Explanation of Cash Value Life Insurance 106
An Introduction to Cash Value Life Insurance 106
What is Cash Value Insurance versus Term Life Insurance? 110
What Types of Permanent Life Insurance Have Cash Value? 114
How Can My Cash Value Life Insurance Make Me Money? 126
The Bottom Line… Is Cash Value Life Insurance Right for You? 145

INTRODUCTION

How do you grow your money through investments? Many individuals are aware that they could invest for retirement through their company's 401(k) or through an IRA from an outside financial advisor. These are hassle-free, basic options that provide a lucrative nest egg in our retirement years. But, did you know you could have both a 401(k) and IRA at the same time, working for you? What about using a Health Savings Account as an investment tool? Or even selling or renting out your home, all for investment purposes? Finally, have you heard the term municipal bond? There are many other investment vehicles out there in which you can invest and grow your money. This book will discuss five basic options (and three more complex options) to help you decide where you can make the most money. First, let's start with the basics! The following basic investment options will be discussed:

Basic Options:
1. 401(k) and IRAs
2. Investing in a Health Savings Account
3. Selling Your Home
4. Renting Your Home for 14 Days or Less
5. Benefits of Investing in Municipal Bonds

BASIC OPTION 1: 401K or IRA? Why Not Both!

If you are not ready to enter the confusion of the stock market, opening a 401(k) and an Individual Retirement Account (IRAs) are two of the most common investment vehicles you can use to save for retirement. Both options offer tax benefits and are flexible as to how much you must contribute each month. And, you can have both at the same time accumulating funds towards your retirement.

Many people either have one investment plan or the other, depending on what their employers offer as a retirement option. However, you may be unaware that you can have a 401(k) through your employer and also have an IRA as another option to save for retirement. When an employer offers a 401(k) to its employees, it will often match the employee's contributions up to a certain percentage. This does not always happen and is not required, but if the employer does offer a contribution match, you should definitely take advantage of this extra money. It is basically like having a tax-deferred savings account that is easy – it is tax-deferred through automatic payroll deduction – and gives you free money if your employer offers a match. What if your employer does not offer a contribution match? You probably want to start with an IRA for your retirement savings, max out that option, and then look into other options that can grow your money tax-free with a hefty return on investment.

Below will review the basics of each option along with the pros and cons of each. As the Vanguard information states above, if your company offers a matched 401(k), you are giving up free money if you do not take advantage of that investment option. But, there are other times in which an IRA is a lucrative retirement savings option as well. Although both types of retirement plans offer tax benefits and savings options, there are some important differences one must weigh in order to make an education decision on where to put your extra cash.

401(k)

A 401(k) is a retirement savings plan that is offered by an employer so that employees can save and invest a portion of their paycheck each month and accumulate monies for their future. Probably the greatest benefit of using a 401(k) for retirement savings is the convenience and ease because it is set up by your employer. A 401(k) is a tax-deferred retirement savings account that most employers offer as a benefit for their employees. You can decide how much you want to put in each month, usually a chosen percentage of your salary, and then your employer may also choose how much additional money the company will also contribute to your retirement plan.

Contributions are made pre-tax, which means the IRS will not tax you on these monies when you are doing your taxes each year. That is, the money you contribute to your 401(k) lowers your taxable income each year, dollar for dollar. This is a great way to lower your tax bill or raise your tax refund. It really just depends on how much you can afford to contribute each year to your 401(k) plan. For example, most 401(k) plans allow employers to contribute up to 6% of an employee's salary. So, you would need to calculate what this number would be based on your salary and then decide if you can give up those monies for your retirement and the maximum employee match. For example, if your annual salary is $50,000 and you decide to put in 3% of that salary per year, you are contributing $1,500, tax free, through automatic payroll deduction. If your company also offers a match, they will then also put in $1,500 because they will meet that 3% cap. Now, if they only will match up to 3% and you put in more than $1,500, they will not match more than the original amount you contributed. Therefore, always research your company's contribution matching funds to make sure you know what amount or percentage will qualify.

Company 401(k) plans are an easy and convenient way to save for retirement because you do not need to do a thing! Usually, an employer will use an outside company to take care of the monies and control how your money is invested. Most plans usually spread out your contributions throughout a spread of mutual funds that are comprised of stocks, bonds, and money market investments. This outside company will deposit the monies in these various investments on your behalf and help make sure they grow productively. Then, the investment income accrues and compounds tax-free because of the tax-deferred growth on investment gains. All of these contributions are held in a single plan trust, with each employee's individual plan being tracked separately and then noted on tax forms each year. However, how much you put into your 401(k) each year should really depend on whether or not your company matches these funds and, if they do, how much of a match they give you.

Company match: If your employer offers a 401(k) that has a company match, you should fund your 401(k) to its maximum contribution point so that you can get the most matching dollars from your employer. This is free money from your employer that you should not pass up! Basically, a guaranteed return on your investment! Then, you can put any additional funds towards retirement into an IRA. You can check your employee benefits handbook to see if your employer matches any portion of money you contribute to your 401(k) and how much.

How does your company determine what to match? It really is up to the employer. They may contribute a certain percentage of your annual salary, whether it is 3%, 6%, or sometimes even 100%! The employer may also decide to match the contributions up to a certain dollar amount each year, regardless of what your annual income is, which then would limit their accountability to highly-compensated employees whose percentage would be much higher otherwise. For example, an employer may decide to match the first $5,000 of an employee's contributions. If that employee's annual income was $200,000, that would be much more lucrative to the employer than matching 3%, which would end up being a $6,000 contribution, or 6%, which would add up to a hefty $12,000 contribution for the employer.

NOTE: The monies that your employer contributes to your 401(k) DO NOT count towards the 401(k) contribution limits. For 2019, these limits are $19,000 with an additional "catch-up" contribution limit for those ages 50 and over remaining at $6,000, totaling $25,000. Therefore, if you made $19,000 per year and were under the age of 50, you could technically invest all of your salary into your 401(k).

No company match: If your employers does not offer a company match for your 401(k), you should probably put your retirement monies into an IRA first and then, after reaching your IRA's contribution limit, fund your 401(k) with the rest of the money you've allocated towards retirement. The contribution limits are higher for 401(k) plans than IRAs, with the total for 2019 being $56,000 ($62,000 for those 50 and older due to the additional $6,000 catch-up contribution). However, an IRA offers an unlimited amount of investment options, which could give you the ability to shop for investment funds that give you more risk (and more reward!). So, you should first max out your IRA contributions and then work towards the 401(k) limit.

There is a salary cap at $280,000 when determining your annual contributions as well as your employers. Your earnings are never counted towards this cap. In addition, your employer may have its own rules on when you could begin seeing a company match in your 401(k), such as being with the company a minimum of three years.

What about vesting? After you have determined whether or not your company will match your own 401(k) contributions, you should also be familiar with your plan's vesting schedule. In the simplest of terms, vesting dictates who exactly owns a percentage (or all) the 401(k) at a certain point in time. Usually, an employee will vest (i.e., own) a certain percentage of your 401(k) account each year until you work at the job for a designated amount of time. Therefore, if an employee is 100% vested, this means the employer owns 100% of the account and the employer cannot take back any of those monies if the employee quits. One-hundred percent of the money is the employees and he or she can take it with him or her after leaving the job. However, sometimes it takes time for an employee to be 100% vested. Therefore, you need to know when you become 100% vested. If you do not, you may forfeit some or all of your employer's contributions if you quit your job too early. If you do not think you are going to be at that job for a certain amount of time, you should consider other savings options other than an employer-matching

401(k), especially if it takes a longer period of time to become 100% vested into the savings program.

So basically, vesting means you actually own the 401(k). Once you are 100% vested in your account, you own 100% of it and the employer cannot forfeit – or take back – the monies the company matched for any reason. For example, some companies make you work a minimum of five years before you are "vested" into the 401(k), while other companies may have a lower three-year minimum. How does this work? Take this example: an employer has an employer-contribution 401(k) retirement plan, but has a six-year vesting schedule that is based on a full calendar year. Stephanie begins working in June 2014 and quits in August 2018. She has worked the minimum amount of hours required under the plan each year; therefore, she earned five years of vesting into the plan, which would equate to 80% of those monies being vested in her account.

That being said, you, the employee, will ALWAYS own 100% of what you, yourself, put into your 401(k) account.

When can I withdraw my 401(k) funds?

This is a common question most employees do not the answer to as they are contributing their funds towards retirement each paycheck. As long as you do not withdraw your retirement monies until after you are age 59 ½, withdraws are taxed at the normal tax rate. You may be able to take out a loan or a hardship withdrawal before reaching this age, which is an emergency withdraw from your 401(k). However, these monies taken out before you reach 59 ½ are usually subject to a 10% IRS early withdrawal penalty as well as the normal income taxes. Remember that loans from 401(k)'s are paid back, but hardship withdrawals are not. No matter what, you are required to take distributions from your 401(k) once you turn age 70 ½.

401(k) plans are not free and there is usually a small cost associated with having your employer handle the plan. Also remember that if you leave your company, you can no longer contribute to the company-owned 401(k). However, you can roll those monies over into an IRA plan. And, an IRA usually has much smaller costs associated with the handling of those accounts.

IRA

An IRA is a retirement account that is not connected to your employer. Instead, you would set up your own IRA with an outside financial advisor and then determine how much you would like to contribute to that retirement account each month. You can also rollover monies from an old 401(k) into a personal IRA. The financial advisor invests your money in stocks and bonds on your behalf in order for you to get the most return on this investment.

The contribution limit for an IRA is $6,000 per year, plus a $1,000 catch-up contribution for those age 50 and older. As discussed above, there are many more investment options with an IRA, which means there are more ways to accrue money through this retirement option. You may choose from an unlimited amount of stocks, bonds, CDs, and possibly even real estate options in which to invest your money.

If you are interested in investing your retirement monies into an IRA, you will need to understand the difference between a traditional and Roth IRA plan:

Traditional IRAs: This type of retirement option allows you to contribute pretax income into your investments that will grow tax-deferred. If you would like a tax break upfront, then a traditional IRA is the right choice. However, check if you also have a 401(k) because your IRA tax deduction could be reduced or eliminated depending on your income. This is because each year the government places contribution limits on IRAs depending on what your adjusted gross income (AGI) is on your tax return. Your AGI is basically your gross income you earned during the calendar year shown on line 22 (in 2018) on the Form 1040, minus any deductions you could take on lines 23 through 36. These deductions could range from educator expenses for those teaching in grades kindergarten through twelfth grade; health savings account deductions; certain moving expenses; and student loan interest, college tuition, and college fees deductions. Sometimes, these deductions can greatly reduce one's AGI and allow him or her to contribute more to an IRA. This is why it is so important to understand how to find your AGI on your tax return – each year the government allocates stiff contribution limits depending on what your AGI was for that year.

The traditional IRA contribution limit for 2019 is $6,000 ($7,000 if you are age 50 or older). You can deduct your IRA contributions on your tax return whether you itemize deductions or take the standard deduction. However, the IRS imposes "phase-out ranges" for income limits as follows for 2019:

Married filing jointly:
- Full deduction if your modified AGI is $103,000 or less
- Partial deduction if your modified AGI is more than $103,000 but less than $123,000
- No deduction if your modified AGI is more than $123,000

Married filing jointly if your spouse is covered by a work retirement plan:
- Full deduction if your modified AGI is $193,000 or less
- Partial deduction if your modified AGI is more than $193,000 but less than $203,000
- No deduction if your modified AGI is more than $203,000

Single or head of household:

- Full deduction if your modified AGI is $64,000 or less
- Partial deduction if your modified AGI is more than $64,000 but less than $74,000
- No deduction if your modified AGI is more than $74,000

Married filing separately:
- Full deduction is not available
- Partial deduction if your modified AGI is less than $10,000
- No deduction if your modified AGI is more than $10,000

Even if you do not qualify for a tax deduction due to the income limits above, you can still contribute to a traditional IRA. Your investments will grow tax-deferred, which means you won't be taxed on any gains until you withdraw them. Then, retirement distributions are taxed as ordinary income. You can make an early withdraw before age 59 ½, but this would be subject to income tax and a 10% penalty.

Although there are income limits on whether or not you can take a tax deduction on your traditional IRA contributions, there are no income limits on anyone who would like to open and contribute to a traditional IRA. You can also use traditional IRA money to pay for qualified college expenses without paying an early distribution penalty (but you will pay taxes on the distribution). Finally, another major benefit of a traditional (and Roth) IRA is that you can also use up to $10,000 from a traditional IRA towards the purchase of your first home without a withdrawal penalty, and will just owe taxes on the distribution.

If you decide to open a traditional IRA, please note that you will be required to take distributions at age 70 ½ and will no longer make contributions after turning that age.

Roth IRAs: If you do not need the upfront tax break from a traditional IRA, you can contribute to a Roth IRA and withdraw the monies tax-free when it is time to retire. This means all of your contributions and investment earnings that accumulated over time come out tax free, a great benefit if you can wait for those tax-free options later in life. However, this means your contributions each year cannot be deducted on your tax bill.

A Roth IRA is also a great retirement choice if you are not eligible to deduct traditional IRA contributions because of the phase-out ranges listed above. In addition, Roth IRAs are not affected by your participation in a company-owned 401(k), as are traditional IRAs.

Similar to traditional IRAs, the Roth IRA contribution limit for 2019 is $6,000 ($7,000 if you are age 50 or older). You can use a Roth IRA in addition to your 401(k), but you are not eligible for a Roth IRA is you earn too much money. The IRS imposes contribution limits as follows for 2019:

Married filing jointly or qualifying widow(er):
- If your modified AGI is $193,000 or less, your maximum contribution is $6,000 ($7,000 if you are age 50 or older)
- If your modified AGI is more than $193,000 but less than $202,999, the contribution is reduced
- If your modified AGI is more than $203,000, you are not eligible to make contributions

Single, head of household, or married filing separately if you did not live with your spouse in 2019:
- If your modified AGI is $122,000 or less, your maximum contribution is $6,000 ($7,000 if you are age 50 or older)
- If your modified AGI is more than $122,000 but less than $136,999, the contribution is reduced
- If your modified AGI is more than $137,000, you are not eligible to make contributions

Age 59 ½ is also the magic number for withdrawing Roth IRA distributions, as long as your held the account for at least five years, without paying federal taxes.

A Roth IRA will work best for someone who does not need to touch his or her contributions until retirement since this plan offers tax-free withdrawals of earnings after you retire. This really is the largest benefit to a Roth IRA; if you do not need the monies right away, keep them safe and sound, and tax-free, in this account until you need to use this nest egg for retirement.

In addition, a Roth IRA may even give more flexibility on investments than a 401(k) in certain situations. For example, if investors contribute after-tax dollars from their paycheck to a Roth IRA account, they can withdraw those monies at any time without owing tax on them because essentially they were already taxed before being contributed. However, that only counts towards the contributions, not the earnings (what those contributions are making from the Roth IRA investment). You need to make sure you do not withdraw those funds before reading 59 ½ years of age. So, if this same investor withdraws the account earnings after age 59 ½ (we are assuming the account is at least five years old, as discussed above), those earnings are tax free. Compared to the 401(k) discussed earlier, this ability to have tax-free withdrawals is probably the biggest benefit of having a Roth IRA instead of a 401(k) retirement plan. In addition, you can withdraw Roth IRA money early without penalty to pay for qualified college expenses or use the monies to supplement a college savings account like a 529 plan. However, you will owe income taxes on these early distributions even if the earnings are used for qualified college expenses.

To sum up, a Roth IRA does give investors much more flexibility than a traditional 401(k) plan. Although both plans do invest monies into mutual funds, 401(k) plans are usually more limited as to what funds you can invest in versus the wider variety of choices for a Roth IRA. If you would like more control over where your money is being invested, and you do not need the monies until retirement, you should chose a Roth IRA.

BASIC OPTION 2: Investing in a Health Savings Account

Most individuals have a basic understanding of why they should have a 401(k) and an IRA for their retirement, yet a Health Savings Account (HSA) is sometimes forgotten when one is investing in retirement. You might have an understanding of how an HSA can helpyou're your medical bills using tax-free funds. However, a HSA is also an investment option that is kind of like a "Health IRA," which supplements the retirement benefits of the 401(k) and IRA very well.

What is an HSA?

A HSA is a savings and investing account that individuals can use to save money for health care, tax free, as long as they are enrolled in a high deductible health insurance plan (HDHP). HDHP's tend to scare people away from having an HSA due to the very high deductibles that come with this type of insurance plan. But, one benefit of having a HDHP is that the monthly premiums are usually lower than a traditional health plan. However, some people still shy away from HDHP's because of the higher deductible you need to pay before the insurance part kicks in and starts covering expenses. This because health savings accounts are only available to certain health insurance plans that meet specific criteria, and one of those criterion is a higher deductible, which is the money you will pay out of pocket for your health care before your insurance plan kicks in and starts paying those health care bills ($1,300 for individuals and $2,600 per family).

Even with the higher deductible, the money you save on the monthly premiums and tax benefits makes up for those out-of-pocket expenses. And, the money you put into your HSA is meant to cover just that – your deductible and any unforeseen out-of-pocket expenses that may arise.

The tax benefits are three-fold when you choose to use an HSA. First, you are not taxed when you put money into a HSA, which means those monies could possibly drop your income to a lower tax bracket when tax time comes. In fact, Michael Kitces (July 4, 2018), director of financial planning at Pinnacle Advisory Group, Inc. in Columbia, Maryland, said "the triple-tax-free Health Savings Account is the most tax-preferred account available!" (Tier 1 section, para. 5). What is this triple-tax-free aspect that is so beneficial to investors? When you contribute to a HSA, you get a tax-deduction upfront because the money you are investing will not be taxed by the IRS on your tax return for that year (first tax-free benefit). Then, the monies you invest into the HSA will grow tax-deferred over time (second tax-free benefit). Finally, the money will end up being tax free when distributed for medical-related expenses (third tax-free benefit). Thus, the triple-tax-free benefits of an HAS.

In 2019, individuals can contribute up to $3,500 and families can contribute up to $7,000 (compared to the $6,000 maximum for IRAs). There is also a $1,000 catch-up contribution for those age 55 and older (similar to the IRA previously discussed). And, anyone can contribute to your HSA as long as it does not exceed the IRS-stipulated limits.

You can even have your contributions deducted from your payroll so that lowering your taxes is even easier. For example, if you and your spouse make a combined total of 164,000, in 2019 you would be taxed at the 32% tax rate. However, if you contributed the maximum $7,000 into your HAS from your paycheck, this would bring your taxable income down to $157,000, which is taxed at a much lower 24% tax rate. So, you are not just saving for your future, but also saving on your tax bill.

But, the tax benefits don't stop there! Your money that is in the HSA also grows tax-free, and when you take the money out for medical expenses you are again not taxed on those withdrawals. So, a HSA definitely offers a three-fold benefit when you think of taxes! Some qualified medical expenses could include, but are not limited to:

- Emergency room visits
- Co-payments
- Insurance deductibles
- Dental visits
- Eye exams and glasses
- Medicare premiums
- Prescriptions
- X-rays
- Mental health services
- In-home nursing care or nursing home payments

Many people get confused with the fact that you don't have a time limit in which to spend your HSA funds because they get them confused with a Flexible Spending Account (FSA). An FSA is another tax-free option to save for medical expenses throughout the year. FSAs are usually offered by employers' health insurance plans and allow employees to contribute tax-free monies into an account for medical bills. However, an FSA has a "use it or lose it" approach; if you don't spend the monies in that calendar year, they are lost. This is not the case for an HSA. The money you put into your HSA is completely yours, whether you don't spend it during the calendar year you put it in or even if you leave your job and get a new one (and new health plan). You can roll the money from your old HSA into your new one and not lose a penny! Then, those monies will continue to roll over year after year so you still have access to all of your hard earned money that you've put into your account.

Basically, you can invest into an HSA over time and leave those monies to grow over the long term until you need them. Because there is no minimum distribution for an HSA, you can keep the money in this investment plan for as long as you'd like until you need to use them. This is because HSA's do not have a "use it or lose it" requirement, which would mean you would have to cover medical expenses with those monies the same year you contribute to the plan. Instead, HSA monies can be used in the future. So, many individuals who use their HSA for an investment plan contribute monies with the sole purpose of NOT using those monies until retirement. Instead, they pay their medical expenses out of pocket and then let the HSA grow (tax-free) like a traditional retirement plan.

This is what makes an HSA basically a "health IRA" – you can use the monies you invest for anything you like and pay taxes on the withdrawals, similar to a traditional IRA. However, if you use those funds for medical purposes, then the withdrawals are tax free! This benefit is extremely important when saving for retirement since, as we get older, our medical bills tend to increase over time. You may need more medications, more doctors' visits, and even possibly more testing and surgeries. With an HSA that is an investment option that has been accumulating over time, you will now have tax-free monies in which to pay for these possible medical issues.

An HSA is two-fold: it allows you to save for retirement, with those withdrawals being taxed like an IRA, but also allows you to plan ahead to pay for future health costs tax free. After you retire, a HSA can help you pay for doctors' visits, prescriptions, and any other medical needs tax-free, while also giving you the addition funds to support your retirement needs.

Once you turn age 65, the HSA will act like a traditional IRA, but you also become eligible for Medicare coverage after this birthday. Although you can no longer contribute to your HSA if you enroll in Medicare, because it is not a HDHP, you can still use the money you had invested in your HSA tax-free for any out-of-pocket medical expenses. In fact, you can even use those monies to pay your Medicare premiums! In addition, you can withdraw the money without being penalized after you turn 65 and will just need to pay taxes on the withdrawal. However, if you withdrawal these funds and use them for nonqualified medical expenses before you turn 65, they will be taxed as income and be subject to a 20% penalty.

With the money in the account, you can save it like a savings account, but you can also invest it. Unlike an FSA, which has annual limits on how much you can put into the account, an HSA can continue to grow throughout your contributions, through investing, or through a combination of both.

How to Turn a HSA Into an Investment Vehicle

When you first open an HSA, it will act as a savings account that earns interest as you contribute monies each month. However, once you reach a certain balance you can alter your HSA so that it acts as an investment account like a traditional IRA.

Similar to an IRA, contributions to your HSA are tax free and the money grows over time also tax free. This includes any interest, dividends, or capital gains, they are all nontaxable. If you withdraw the funds for everyday purchases, you will pay taxes on those withdrawals just like an IRA. However, you can withdraw the money tax free for qualifying medical expenses. This is what makes an HSA so much more superior to a 401(k) or IRA; we will all eventually have medical expenses, and you can pay for them with tax-free money. And, you can withdraw all of the money penalty-free after the age of 65. So, right now it sounds a lot like a traditional IRA that simply gives you tax-free benefits for paying for medical expenses.

Since an HSA an IRA have so many similarities, you should treat it like an investment vehicle meant to accumulate long-term growth. You need to maximize your contributions early (for example, contributing the maximum contribution of $7,000 in 2019) and withdrawal the funds later, probably not for years and years. This is how you make the HSA work as a proper investment tool. In fact, if you can contribute to your HSA but still pay your current medical expenses out of pocket, you will build your investment more over the years. This is because if you take out your HSA monies to pay for early medical expenses, those contributions won't compound sufficiently with the market over time. Let the investments pay off for you, which usually only happen after the long haul when you let your investments grow over time.

If you find out your current HSA doesn't have investing capabilities, or the fees are too expensive to invest, you can simply leave that provider and find another one that fits your investment needs even if you have an employer-backed HSA. Or, you can have more than one HSA as long as you do not exceed the annual contribution limits.

Just remember that the only caveat to having an HSA is that you must be enrolled in a high deductive health plan. This could be problematic to some individuals or families who may not be able to afford the larger deductible, even with lower monthly premiums. One hospital visit could cost thousands of dollars out of pocket, making it tempting to dip into the HSA. But, if you can afford to put as much as you can into an HSA while still affording the higher deductibles of your health plan and paying some of your medical expenses out of pocket, you could have a very large chunk of change in this additional investment plan when it comes to retirement.

Your goal should be to boost your HSA funds as much as possible over time, try not to withdrawal too much over the course of your investment, and then have a nice nest egg for either your medical bills (tax free) in your older age or a nice amount of money for other retirement purposes. Unlike an FSA, which has the "use it or lose it" stipulation, your HSA money lasts forever until you decide to withdrawal it. So, you should be sure to invest your HSA money when the time comes; just don't use it as a savings account because it is so much more!

In the end, you can have a well-balanced and very lucrative retirement plan if you have a 401(k), an IRA, and a HSA complementing one another throughout your life. Therefore, you should invest your money in the HSA similar to how you would your 401(k) and IRA. It is also important to note that the IRS allows you to transfer funds from your IRA to your HSA once in your lifetime, so this could be an option if more medical bills arise later in life or if an unexpected hospital trip occurs while you are still saving. In the end, it make be more cost-effective to dip into your IRA tax free through a transfer than putting a large medical bill on a credit card.

No matter what, make sure you are using a financial adviser who has an understanding of your investment strategies and goals and what you would like to achieve financially later in life.

BASIC OPTION 3: Selling Your Home

Not many home buyers have making money in their minds when purchasing a home, but what if you could turn your home into an investment option to make money? You can definitely turn your home into a money-maker, but it isn't easy. There are many steps you need to take to make sure you're getting the biggest "bang for your buck." However, maybe sellers don't realize that some of these steps may cost quite a bit of money, so you first need to make sure you understand how much it actually costs to sell a home. Then, you can begin the process of upgrading, finding an agent, and going through the other steps in the selling process.

Below are 6 steps to make sure your home sales leaves you with the most money:

1. Know how to choose the right time to sell
2. Understand your market, your neighborhood, your buyer
3. How much will my home sale cost?
4. Adding value through renovations.
5. Contact a real estate agent

6. Set the right price and negotiate the best offer

1. Know How to Choose the Right Time to Sell:

Before you make any other decisions about selling your home, you need to set a sale date. That way, you have a deadline in which you need to get everything else done to get the biggest investment out of your sale. But, when exactly is the right time to sell? There are thing things you should think about when setting this date: The seasons, your home equity, and your overall life decisions.

If you are not pressed for time or money, the best time to sell a home is in spring or summer because prices are at their highest during these months. This is because those are the seasons that families usually want to move – they aren't dealing with snow and sleet, kids are out of school or winding down, and this means you can sell your home at its peak value. However, some experts have claimed sellers do not to worry about selling only in the warmer months (usually April to June). Some real estate experts have actually claimed that the "off months" – December, January, February, and March – may net more for homes than the summer months because there is not as much competition from other sellers! So, the less homes that are on the market means the sale price of your home could actually go up because there are not a lot of homes to choose from! Therefore, do not feel the need to rush to get your home ready to sell just because the warm weather could bring out those buyers.

After calculating whether you are going to sell during the warmer months or wait until the competition wanes down in the fall, you then need to find out how much equity you have in your home to pay off the selling costs and still put money in your pocket. If you choose to use a realtor (discussed below) then you will have realtor feels, home repairs, your mortgage payoff, and pricey closing costs and other additional fees. Most homeowners will not build up enough equity in their home until living in it for at least five years. However, if you have refinanced your home for a better rate over the years, this could also hurt your chances to make the most money off of a sale.

Life is also a consideration of when to sell. Are you starting a new job, is your child starting college, are you taking care of aging parents? These are also considerations when thinking about how to make the most money on your home sale.

Once you decide the when, you can then do your research on the local real estate market to continue building your investment options.

2. Understand Your Market, the Economy, Your Neighborhood, Your Buyer

Although the Internet has given us access to home sales around the world, you really need to be comparing your home sale to your own neighborhood, not one miles away. Just because a home with the same amount of bedrooms, bathrooms, and square feet is selling for $500,000 in California, doesn't mean your same home will go for that price. Researching your own neighborhood is a good sign of whether there are more homes for sale than buyers – you don't want your home to be stuck in the "buyers' market." Instead, you want more buyers than homes for sale, which will drive up your asking prices as the buyers compete for fewer homes on the market. You want a "sellers' market."

A great way to gauge whether you're entering a buyers' or sellers' market is to find out what similar homes are selling for in your area. Web sites like Zillow, Trulia, and Realtor.com can give you a great idea of what similar homes are selling for and how long they are on the market. Is it worth adding upgrades if similar homes don't have them? Maybe not. How long have other homes in your neighborhood been listed, for example? Have the sales prices gone down? Looking at the rate in which home prices are appreciating will show how fast home prices are rising and whether or not buyers will be willing to pay more for your home. This can give you an idea on the demand for sales and how much buyers may be willing to negotiate.

The economy will also drive home sales and even the price of what you can get for your home. Traditionally, your home's value will more than likely increase around 3 to 4% in a strong economy due to the standard inflation rises as well as population growth during a sounder economy. Therefore, as a seller you should do your research to see how homes are selling during the current economy, possibly reviewing the S&P CoreLogic Case-Shiller National Home Price Index (which can be found here: https://us.spindices.com/indices/real-estate/sp-corelogic-case-shiller-us-national-home-price-nsa-index).

You also need to do a little research on your ideal homebuyer for your specific house. Different properties will attract different homebuyers; for example, a younger couple with a baby will be looking for much different things than a married couple in their thirties or forties with older children. Some families want a home to be "move-in ready," while others will be willing to make the appropriate repairs or changes in aesthetics. Knowing who exactly your target buyer is will make a huge difference when selling your home.

3. How Much Will My Home Sale Cost?

Remember, selling a house will cost money out-of-pocket, and it's important to understand those numbers before putting your home on the market. You will make this money back in the sale, but that may not happen for months. There are so many factors to consider: real estate commissions, closing costs, seller concessions and contingencies, maintenance and repairs, etc. All of these expenses will be taken either out of pocket or from the sales price of your home.

For example, a real estate agent usually gets between 5-6% of your sales price, while closing costs usually are around 1% of the sale. Sellers may also have concessions – a new roof, a new water heater, etc. This could add another 1.5-2% into your expenses. However, hiring a home inspector early (another added expense) could keep these concessions to a minimum.

If you take control of getting a pre-sale home inspection, it will ultimately give you more control when the seller begins trying to make costly concessions and contingencies. You want to discover and handle any problems before your sale! Therefore, a pre-listing inspection can give you the opportunity, early, to discover any unforeseen problems and take care of them before you put your home on the market.

You also need to make sure you're "staging" your home so that it looks lived in but not cluttered. That is, clean the refrigerator of all those magnets and pictures your kids made, pack away your child's doll collection, and organize your closets to maximize space. You want your home to look both well-maintained and move-in ready. For example, an organized and clean home illustrates to a potential buyer that the house has been well-maintained while still giving off a homey, lived-in atmosphere. A well-furnished room is much more attractive to buyers than an empty room that doesn't look lived in or welcoming to guests. Below is a list of some home upgrades and repairs that can put more money into your pocket down the road.

4. Adding Value Through Renovations

You can add considerable value to the sale price of your home by competing both exterior and interior renovations. Do not just rush to put your house on the market because the economy is strong or homes in your area are being picked up left and right. You need to make sure you make the proper home renovations and repairs so that you can get the best price for your home.

Exterior:

Studies have shown that you will have a higher rate of return focusing on updating the exterior of your home rather than the interior. For example, garage door replacement has had the highest average return on investment, recouping nearly 100% of what it costs during the resale of a home. This same return on investment is usually true for all of your "curb appeal."

Adding a wood deck will also increase your home's value, while also giving your own family outside living space throughout the year. A wood deck can cost anywhere from $5,000-$12,000 depending on the size and materials. However, exterior upgrades so not have to be so elaborate; for example, repainting the exterior of your home gives it a new, fresh look for under $1,000.

Landscaping also does wonders to any home. Trimming hedges and trees, having a well-cut lawn, quality furniture and eye-catching flowers can increase a sales price anywhere from 5% to 13%. In fact, Jamie Wiebe (May 5, 2016), a writer for Realtor.com, stated that "Good landscaping can add up to 28% to overall home value. Why pass up free money?" (para. 4).

Interior:
Kitchen remodeling has nearly the same rate of return as exterior projects, as sellers usually get about 80-90% of their money back from a kitchen renovation. This includes upgrading kitchen appliances (stainless steel rank highest), staging an eat-in area with a set table and new linens, and painting the walls lighter, brighter colors. A new floor also adds value to your new, lived-in kitchen. If you have extra funds to invest into this upgrade, granite countertops are also a solid addition that adds value to the sales price. Although upgrading your countertops may cost a few thousand dollars, a seller may ask between $5,000-$10,000 of the original asking price if the kitchen doesn't impress them. However, it could be as

inexpensive and simple as installing new hardware on the cabinets and doors to spruce up your home.

A close second to renovating your kitchen is your bathroom. Bathroom renovations do not have to be costly; replacing hardware in the vanity, bath and shower, repainting and updating lighting can increase your sales price around 4%, according to a Cost v. Value report. No matter what, if you want to get the best bang for your buck, the best areas to renovate are definitely the kitchen and the bathroom. Those improvements have been shown to attract buyers and add value to your home more than any other area. Why? We spend most of our lives in these two areas of the house! Home buyers will try to see themselves in both the kitchen and bath rather than other areas of the house. Another reason the kitchen and bath are so worthy for renovating is because buyers look at them as the most time-consuming and costly renovations to do on their own. No one wants to hire a plumber, redo a bath or shower, or have to replace aging kitchen appliances. If a buyer can walk in and see a ready-to-move in kitchen and bath, they may be willing to pay more for your home. In fact, a Harrisburg, Pennsylvania home buyer recently said she almost did not purchase her home just because the kitchen appliances were out of date! It did not matter that the home had a pool and beautiful landscaping – the kitchen appliances alone were almost a deal breaker.

Other overall home improvements include repainting your entire home using neutral colors, such as beiges and off-whites for brightness. Paint the whole house, including the walls, ceilings, and trim. Updating the flooring in your home to hardwood works wonders for buyers that carpet just does not do. Although carpeting was a 1980s and 1990s sensation, carpeting today can actually turn away buyers who cannot see beyond the outdated look of carpeting. Ripping up carpeting and adding either hard wood or Pergo flooring yourself (or even just cleaning and refurbishing what was underneath your carpeting!) could help bring in buyers.

Some other easy tricks to raise that asking price is modernizing lighting and even installing ceiling fans and smart home technology can vastly increase your asking price with inexpensive upfront costs.

Although upgrading everything is tempting, it is important to not over-upgrade! You won't get your money back making huge improvements, but a fresh coat of paint, a new appliance here and there, and bright, fresh lighting will do wonders to your asking price!

Remember...the first impression is the ONLY impression!

Now that you have your house sale ready, the next question to answer is an important one: do you use a real estate agent or complete the sale yourself? The real estate agent will more than likely be the biggest price-tag when you are selling a home, but there is a reason for that price.

5. Contact a Real Estate Agent:

The biggest expense that you will spend from the sale of your home will be paying the real estate agent commission, which usually ends up being between 5-6% of your sale (although some agents do negotiate their commission). That means the sale of a $250,000 home would give $15,000 to the agent for a 6% commission! This makes the "sale by owner" option very tempting to house sellers. However, you are assuming that you have the same knowledge of home sales as a real estate agent, and more than likely you don't. A real estate agent brings the proper education and experience to the complex process of selling a home. This is because your home is more than likely the biggest investment you will ever have – more than your car – and you want to make sure the sale of this important investment is handled properly. Although keeping the stiff agent commission for yourself and putting that "Sale by Owner" sign in your front yard is tempting, you will more than likely still be leaving more money on the table if you go at it by yourself. For example, last year the standard single-family home sold by an agent sold for nearly $60,000 more than the sale by owner homes. That gain is much, much more than the commission percentage a real estate agent would earn from your sale!

Selling a home is more than putting a sign up in the front yard and waiting for buyers to knock on the door. There is scheduling showings, listing the home on the Web, paperwork, pricing, negotiating, just to name a few things in this complicated process.

You want an agent who is tech savvy and has a strong understanding of the multiple listing service (MLS), which is a massive online database that contains listings from across the United States. Thousands of potential buyers have access the MLS for free and most real estate agents are proficient in listing properties and keeping these listings fresh for potential buyers. However, most sale by owner options don't have access to MLS or a broker's contacts and buyers are usually more comfortable dealing with a professional.

Selling a home is time consuming and stressful, and a real estate agent can take the time and stress off your hands and place ads, schedule tours, and keep the MLS up-to-date on your behalf. A real estate agent can help you with all of this and even help you set the right price and negotiate this price with sellers based on the most recent market data.

6. Set the Right Price and Negotiate the Best Offer

You can do your own research about pricing and even get your home appraised for anywhere between $250 and $500 to set your selling price correctly. If the market is good, you can set your sales price around 10-15% above your appraisal. However, if you end up overpricing your home, you may have to drop the price later, which will complicate your sales since buyers may become skeptical as to why you have to drop the price.

This is where your real estate agent comes into play – he or she will suggest not pricing your home too high, but not giving it away from free. You know what investment return you would like to make on the sale, so discuss this number with your agent. When pricing your home, you need to consider all of your renovations as well as your home's location, the schools, the housing market, and the other homes that are selling around you.

Your real estate agent should also help you in the negotiation process, which can sometimes be a stressful back and forth between buyer and seller. Although it may be very tempting to accept the highest offer, remember before we discussed some sellers who would like concessions and contingencies incorporated into the sale. These requests may significantly lower the offer and must be taken into consideration during the negotiating process. For example, some sellers may request financial help with the closing costs, additional repairs to the home, or even ask for brand new appliances and equipment (such as a new water heater or roof!). Your real estate agent will help you navigate through this process as well as research the buyer's themselves – their credit history, income, employment, etc.

Some final thoughts…selling your home can be a very lucrative investment deal, but you need to have an understanding of the best time to sell, your local market trends, and how this will impact the sale price of your home. You don't want to overprice your home, but you don't want to leave money on the table. In the end, this is your money, your investment!

But…selling your home isn't the only option to turn your home into an investment vehicle. You could also rent out your home through sites such as Airbnb, HomeAway, or VRBO.

BASIC OPTION 4: Renting Your Home for 14 Days or Less

If right now isn't a good time for your family to pick up and move, you do have the option of renting out a room, a basement area, or even your entire home for 14 days or less. Why 14 days? As long as you rent out your home for fewer than 15 days, you do not need to report the money earned from your short-term rental as income. Basically, the government still considers a home personal if you live in it more than 14 days, so keep that number in mind!!

NOTE: Airbnb does send tax forms to the IRS documenting the income renters make each year, but as long as you only rent 14 days or less per year you can just explain that your income isn't taxable and attach proof if you're contacted by the IRS.

If you decide to rent out your home for 15 days or more per calendar year, the rent you earn must be included as personal income on your tax return!

Renting out your home, apartment, condo, or even an extra room is a great way to generate additional income. If you live in a vacation hotspot or even just near some popular destinations, you can rent out your home or a portion of your home for anywhere from three days to two weeks and pocket this funds.

Short-term tenants usually look for homes through Web sites like Airbnb, Homeaway, or VRBO. Basically, they are online vacation rental companies that allow homeowners to list their homes on their sites for users to find. Your only job is to list your home, upload attractive pictures, and write up the benefits and amenities that make your home more attractive than others listed on the site. These sites deal with finding the tenants (well, the tenants find you through the site), verifying the guests, and protecting you, the host, from property damage through a property damage protection plan.

What should you expect your responsibilities to be when using a rental Web site to list your home? You will need to create your own listing and keep it up-to-date, respond to potential renters questions and concerns, manage your reservation dates and when your property is available, and make sure your house is clean and inviting for your renters.

The first step in your new rental adventure is to take photos and upload them to your chosen Web site. High quality photos are key! These images are the first thing your potential renter will see, so you need to post high quality, high resolution (but also accurate) photographs to make the best first impression possible.

After you post the photos, you need to be strategic when setting your daily or weekly rates. Potential renters will do their homework on where they can get the best vacation deal, so you should do your homework as well. Try searching comparable listings in your city or town to see what other people are charging for their homes. Are you charging much more than them? If you are, you probably will not find a renter. You will also need to decide what fees you would like to include in the rental price and what fees you will charge as extra add-ons, such as a cleaning fee, a late check-in fee, a pet fee (if you allow pets at all!), and any fees for additional days requested late. Most renters make these separate fees, but if you put them into the entire rental fee it could make your rental much more attractive to vacationers looking to stay in your area.

Similar to negotiating the sale of your home, you should do some research as to what similar homes in your area are renting at and then set your home's rental options competitively. But, you'll also need to take into account your own expenses that are included in renting out your home. If you use a Web site such as Airbnb, HomeAway, or VRBO, you need to take into consideration the fees they charge for listing homes and/or processing payments.

The two leading housing platforms for listing short-term rentals in which to choose are Airbnb and VRBO. However, each site is very different in their fee structure. Both Airbnb and VRBO charge host and guest fees, with Airbnb charging guests a 5 to 15% fee on their reservation while hosts are charged a 3% fee for each booking placed through Airbnb ("experiences," however, are charged a 20% service fee on Airbnb). VRBO, on the other hand, charges guests between 6 and 12% on their reservations and then homeowners will pay what is known as a subscription fee to rent their home through this site. As a renter, you can either pay per booking, which means you are charged 8% on each booking you complete through VRBO (recommended for those who are only renting for six weeks or less per year), or an upfront annual subscription payment of $499 (recommended for renters who are hosting their homes year round since this will more than likely be less than the 8% per booking fee). If you are planning on renting out your home, you will need to compare all of these fees, figure out how often you will be renting your home, and then decide which site and which plan is more lucrative to your rental home excursions.

Does your home owner's insurance cover potential losses from renting out your home, such as damage to the property not covered by the hosting Web site or, even worse, if you're sued by the tenants? You'll need to make sure you have the protection before entering into the world of renting out your home. Some home insurance policies cover short-term rentals, but you need to make sure you're protected. In addition, you may need to find out if your city or town allows for short-term rentals.

Remember that tenants can rate you on these sites, and these ratings and comments can make or break your rental future! Make sure your house is cleaned thoroughly, furnished nicely (but not overly expensive!), and has some amenities important to renters – appliances, wifi, clean towels and linens, working smoke detectors, coffee maker, toaster, etc.

Many renters add a cleaning fee into the rental total, but those monies may then be charged a service fee by the Web site you are using. No matter what, your bathrooms and kitchen should be spotless, beds should be made with clean linens, and there shouldn't be any clutter lying around. Any obvious hazards, such as a loose step, exposed wiring, or cracked tiles, should be fixed, and you should never leave any personal valuables out in the home.

In the end, simply be a good host. Fresh flowers, a handwritten note, and a stocked pantry can work wonders for your guests and their later reviews of you. If something isn't working or is broken, don't waste time fixing it and don't give your tenants a hard time.

BASIC OPTION 5: Benefits of Investing in Municipal Bonds

Usually the term "tax-free investing" is nearly impossible to achieve, but this is the main benefit with investing in municipal bonds. If you want a sure-fire way to earn tax-free interest income for retirement, "muni bonds," as they are sometimes called, are the way to go. Municipal bonds are fixed-income investments that accumulate interest that is exempt from federal taxes and, many times, also exempt from state and local taxes. They are issued by local government entities, whether that is a municipality, city, county, or even a state. When you investment your monies into a municipal bond, you will get an interest payment twice a year and then get your initial investment – also called the principal – back to you when your bond matures.

Because municipal bonds may be issued by a state or local municipality, they can be used for a variety of projects such as new roads, bridges, hospitals, even baseball or football stadiums. These types of projects are usually financed through the issuance of municipal bonds, so you can be part of these new projects to better your community.

Unlike corporate bonds, which are issued by large companies yield more interest but are subject to ordinary income taxes, municipal bonds are issued by states, cities, counties, and other governmental entities and earn interest income tax free – you will not owe anything to your state and federal taxes on the interest you make from this investment choice. These are especially attractive to taxpayers in a higher tax bracket, as they would need to pay taxes on corporate bonds at their higher tax rate where as their municipal bonds would not be subject to those tax rates. In addition, bonds are usually considered a safer investment that stocks.

Tax-free earnings is the only attraction to municipal bonds; because they are issued by states, cities, counties, and other governmental entities (unlike corporate bonds that are issued by large companies), the money you spend on these bonds go into local state and government projects that help others. Basically, these types of bonds were started specifically to help fund public works in a local area. The first municipal bond was issued by New York City in 1812 to fudn the digging of a canal, and since then municipal bonds have helped fund San Francisco's Golden Gate Bridge and the Erie Canal.

Your municipal bonds can also give you an emotional as well as financial gain. For example, if you purchase a muni bond from a school district, you are essentially lending money to help that school and then earn tax-free interest on your investment. If your city or town issues the muni bond, your money may go towards fixing roads and bridges, or support hospitals in your area. Essentially, you are loaning them money to help the greater good and they are paying you interest on your loan. Once your bond matures, you are promised the par value of that bond. Because you will get your return on investment in the future, municipal bonds have some very attractive monetary and emotional benefits.

Now, that doesn't mean that municipal bonds don't come without their own set of risks. Although they are safer than stocks, these bonds do still fluctuate with the market (although less frequently and definitely less drastically than stocks do). But, bonds that mature sooner with a shorter duration will fluctuate much less than those with a longer duration that has them mature longer in the future. But…shorter duration bonds always have lower yields than bonds with a longer duration, so there's always a trade-off one way or another.

Because municipal bonds really are a guarantee for solid interest gain, they can be considered a pretty reliable source of ongoing income. Essentially, you are agreeing to invest a certain amount of money into a municipal – a state, city, county, or district, for example – and your principal that you are investing goes into a specific project. Then, the issues agrees to pay you back your investment once your bond matures. But in the meantime, you are collecting interesting payments, tax-free, for as long as you hold your bond.

If you are interested in tapping into this investment option to earn tax-free money, you'll need to understand the difference between the two most common types of municipal bonds:

1. General obligation bonds
2. Revenue bonds

1. General obligation bonds:

These bonds are issued by states, cities, and counties to finance public projects. They are not secured by any assets; that is, they are not linked to a specific revenue stream or fund public projects that make money. Instead, they are specific meant to better the communities they serve, such as improving a school system or building a new playground. These projects don't make anyone money but, instead, are meant to improve the community.

General obligation bonds are backed by what is called a "full faith and credit," which means the issuer (i.e., the city) must do anything it can to pay the bi-yearly interest payments of the bond. For example, some cities have actually raised local taxes to cover the interest payments of outstanding bonds. Therefore, general obligation bonds are usually considered a safer investment than revenue bonds because they are less likely to default on the interest payments. However, since they offer the lowest risk, they usually also offer the lowest yields.

2. Revenue bonds:

These bonds are used to finance public projects and, therefore, are back by revenues from that specific project or source. That is, they have the potential to money. For example, a city might issue revenue bonds to fund the construction of a new bridge on a toll road. The money collected in tolls for those crossing the bridge could then be used to repay the bondholders. However, if those monies don't cover the interest payments, this is when revenue bonds have a higher rate of default than general obligation bonds. That being said, risk also gives more reward since revenue bonds usually offer higher yields than general obligation bonds.

NOTE: There are other types of municipal bonds in which to choose: essential service bonds, anticipation notes, pre-refunded bonds, and insured bonds, to name a few. Speaking with a qualified financial adviser can help you navigate through which municipal bond is right for you and which will give you the most bang for the buck.

How do I invest in municipal bonds?

Municipal bonds do not trade on a centralized exchange like stocks and, instead, trade in a method called "over the counter." This means the transactions are done directly by the buyer and the seller. Maybe there's a program you know of that interests you and is selling bonds for an upcoming project. Or, maybe there are lucrative municipal bonds for sale in your home state. You can do some research to see what is out there. However, not everyone will have the ability to purchase municipal bonds because generally the minimum investment is $5,000.

If you want to purchase a municipal bond, you can either go through a broker who can locate the bonds for you or access the Municipal Securities Rulemaking Board's (MSRB) Electronic Municipal Market Access (EMMA) Web site at https://emma.msrb.org/Home for information about the municipal market. Brokers are required to register with the MSRB and disclose pricing information so that you can figure out if the broker is marking up the bonds incredibly high. However, the EMMA Web site is only for research purposes and does not give buyers an actual platform for purchasing bonds.

If you aren't comfortable going through a broker, you can also invest in municipal bonds by purchasing shares of a mutual fund through your own investment firm. These mutual funds specifically focus on municipal bond investing, which means you can buy a share in many different municipal bonds as opposed to the standard individual or corporate bonds. Going this route will give you diversification in your municipal bond portfolio, and diversifying helps investors avoid losses. A final option for municipal bond purchasing is through an exchange-traded fund, which is a collection of municipal bonds that you can invest in with lower operating expenses. This option may charge lower fees than using a broker or investing in a mutual fund.

How do I make money off of my municipal bonds?

The main way you will grow and earn money through your municipal bonds is through the interest payments you receive (usually twice a year). For example, if you hold onto your municipal bond for 10 years, you will receive 20 tax-free interest payments over the life of that bone. As discussed, this income is not subject to federal tax and, if issued by the state you live in, are also exempt from state and local taxes. For example, if you buy a ten-year, $10,000 bond that pays 4% interest, the issuer is obligated to pay you interest on your principal every six months and then return your original $10,000 once that ten-year period is up. So, because your interest payments are tax free and you are obligated to get your original investment back, it's a win-win.

However, this isn't the only way you can earn money from municipal bonds. You also have the option to sell your bond at a price that's higher than what you initially paid for the bond.

Thinking of the example above, if you purchase a $10,000 bond and then the market value of that bond increases to $13,000, you can sell it for that price and make a profit of $3,000. A bond sale may also be profitable if you purchased your bond at a discount, or below the actual face value of the bond. If you purchased a $10,000 bond on sale for $8,000, for example, you could sell it at the face value and make $2,000 in profits. However, remember that any capital gains on the face value of municipal bonds is not tax free! That is, the $2,000 profit you made on your sale is liable for capital gains taxes on that profit.

Benefits of Municipal bonds:
1. Although corporate bonds may collect higher interest, it is not tax-exempt. Municipal bonds give the investor the ability to collect tax-free interest on a federal level and, in many cases, on the state and local level.
2. Historically, the default rate is low, even with revenue bonds.
3. Your investment goes directly towards improving your community, unlike investing in a corporate bond that just helps that company make more money. Instead, you may be improving a school system, building a new park for children, or improving the local hospital. Just think, you may be able to pat yourself on the back when you drive down that new road your investment helped build!

4. Municipal bonds are sometimes issued with "serial" maturities, which means your bond will have several maturity dates.

However...
1. The tax benefits on municipal bonds is only on the interest payments, not on any potential gains on their face value.
2. The interest gains of municipal bonds are still lower than corporate bonds or stocks. Your municipal bond may also have a lower interest rate than the same type of bond sold to someone else, making yours less competitive.
3. Municipal bonds usually start their investments at a minimum of $5,000, where as corporate bonds could be issued in smaller, $1,000 amounts.
4. Municipal bonds are more complicated to purchase because they are traded on the "over-the-counter" market, where as corporate bonds are listed on exchanges.
5. When you purchase a municipal bond, you are essentially locking a very large amount (at a minimum, $5,000) for an extended period of time. You need to think if that is the best way to handle those monies for that long period of time. What if a more lucrative investment falls into your lap down the road?
6. Although they are safe and default is unlikely, you aren't 100% protected from a municipality defaulting on the bond if they simply cannot make the interest payments. You can

protect yourself, however, by only investing in insured bonds, which offer investors added protection.

If you are considering municipal bonds as a solid investment, you can review the bond rating through the Better Business Bureau or the Moody' report released each year on more than 10,000 municipal bond issuers. In the end, they could be a very lucrative tax-free income source that also helps the community in which you live. As long as you find a municipal bond that has an attractive interest rate and you can hold onto until it matures (that is, you won't need your investment sooner), municipal bonds can be a worthy investment vehicle to grow and earn money.

Time to get a bit more complicated!

Now that you have some basic ideas of where you can invest your monies in order to grow and earn even more cash, we will discuss three more complex options:

1. Cash Value Life Insurance Policies
2. 1031 Exchanges
3. Investing in Qualified Opportunity Zones

COMPLEX OPTION 1: Cash Value Life Insurance Policies

As discussed in section one of this book, there are numerous ways to earn money, invest wisely, and attain tax-free monetary growth. From investing in 401(k)'s, IRAs, and HSAs, to selling or renting out your home, to investing some extra cash in municipal bonds, these are all very simple ways to invest your money easily and pain-free. But, one method many individuals don't know is using cash value life insurance policies to do just this – earn money and attain tax-free growth while investing income wisely.

Cash value life insurance policies do provide the basics of an everyday life insurance plan: they provide monetary coverage while you are living, as well as a death benefit that will go to your loved ones after you die. Each month you pay your premiums similar to term life insurance. However, with a cash value life insurance policy, a portion of your premiums are paid into an investment-type account (i.e., the cash value), while the other portion goes towards death benefits for your beneficiaries. The portion that goes into the investment-type account grows through accruing interest over time (depending on which type of cash value life insurance plan you choose). This cash value is essentially "liquid" and can become a valuable source of income when times are tough or in the case of an emergency.

Although extra cash in your pocket sounds tempting, there is a lot to think about when choosing a cash value insurance policy over the standard term life insurance. First, there are different forms of cash value life insurance in which to choose. Second, cash value life insurance, compared to investing in stocks, usually have a lower rate of return. Third, cash value life insurance has higher premiums, higher fees from the insurance company, and higher commissions from agents.

However, if you do your research and figure out your investment needs, a cash value life insurance plan can become a lucrative savings account that can be used to withdraw funds, attain a loan, or even pay off your very own insurance premiums. It is a great mixture of the simpler investment options we discussed in the first part of this book: a 401(k), IRA, and HSA. Many of the same benefits are available with cash value life insurance, in addition to growing a death benefit that will protect your loved ones after you die.

Yes, the main function of life insurance is to ensure your family's financial well-being after you are no longer there to provide for them financially. Just think of all of the bills you pay every day – mortgage, food, entertainment, college education...the list can go on and on. If you are not there to pay these bills, your life insurance plan is there to replace your income. But, what if you could also benefit from your life insurance plan while you were living? That is what cash value life insurance offers you.

You can withdraw funds or take out a loan in case of an emergency; you can build another nest egg to be used towards your retirement; you can pay off your premiums with the cash invested instead of paying them out of pocket. You can even boost the death benefit for your loved ones more and more with this extra cash. All in all, a cash value life insurance plan allows you to use these funds while you are living, while also protecting those you love after you die. And, all of this is done tax free.

Cash value life insurance is a form of permanent life insurance; that is, it is a policy that provides lifetime coverage and flexibility to cancel your policy, attain the cash value of your policy, or withdraw monies for emergencies. While term life insurance guarantees a death benefit to your beneficiaries at a specific time – your death – permanent life insurance provides coverage and cash value while you are living. As long as the premiums are paid, cash value life insurance provides coverage for your entire life. Term life insurance does not include a cash value, which is why they are usually more affordable than permanent life insurance options.

Cash value life insurance policies usually have higher premiums that term life insurance due to the added lifetime flexibility. That being said, a cash value policy earns interest and defers taxes on these accumulated earnings. The only circumstance in which you could get cash back from a term life insurance policy is if you have a return of premium rider – an add-on policy that returns your premiums you have paid if you outline the term of the policy. Otherwise, if you decide to give you our term life insurance coverage with the insurer, you will not receive anything in return because term life insurance policies do not have a cash value.

So, while your term life insurance provides temporary coverage over a certain period of time – 10, 20, 30, 50 years – it provides no additional cash value. You cannot borrow against a term life policy or cash it in for money when you may need it. This is what makes term life insurance so much more affordable to some people since the premiums are usually lower than permanent life insurance. Although cash value life insurance is pricier, it offers an additional savings component.

Another benefit of cash value life insurance is the stability of the insurance itself. You are going to be insured under the plan in spite of how your health may evolve over time. If your health begins to decline and you have term life insurance, you may need to purchase another term (also called "re-upping" your coverage), which may come with higher premiums when you are at your most vulnerable. This is not the case with cash value life insurance; with this type of policy, you are covered even if your health changes over time. Although you are paying higher premiums with this plan, these premiums remain a flat rate no matter what health issues you may encounter as you get older.

As the policyholder of a cash value policy, you are able to use the cash value of your policy for numerous purposes, whether you need a loan to be paid back at a later date, cash on hand, or even money to help pay your premiums. How does this work?

In order to understand how your cash value life insurance policy would make you money, you need to understand two features offered through a cash value life insurance plan:

1. <u>A death benefit</u> – the amount of money that is paid out to your beneficiaries when you die.
2. <u>Cash value</u> – an investment-like feature that accrues cash to be used in a variety of ways while you are alive.

So, you pay your premiums each month, and then a portion of your premiums are paid into the investment portion of your policy, while the other portion goes into the death benefit for your loved ones protection. The benefits? Tax-free earnings and cash on hand for a variety of options, from withdrawals and loans to paying premiums and saving for retirement:

<u>Tax-free earnings:</u> Probably the best advantage to cash value life insurance is the tax advantage. Similar to other investment options, the cash value of your life insurance policy and the earnings it accrues are tax-free. You can continue to keep these funds tax-free as long as you only withdraw an amount that does not go over what

you have paid in premiums. Therefore, it is recommended to not withdraw more than this amount, as you will have to pay taxes on the difference between what you have already paid in premiums and what amount of cash you are taking out of your policy. The basic rule of thumb is to only make a tax-free withdraw up to the amount you have already paid into the cash-value portion of your insurance policy. If your withdraw exceeds that amount, it will then become taxed income.

Cash on hand: The reason individuals decide to purchase permanent life insurance is because of the cash value. This is the main benefit of cash value life insurance – you have cash on hand if needed while you are living. This is because the cash value element of your policy is basically an investment plan. Therefore, you can do many things with this cash that is similar to a traditional investment tool. The important thing to note, however, is the cash portion of your permanent life insurance plan is a "use it or lose it" scenario. This cash will not be available to your beneficiaries after you die unless you allocate it to the death benefit portion of your plan before your passing.

1. You can simply withdraw the funds, but if the money is not repaid these withdraws will reduce the policy's death benefit;
2. You can take out a loan by borrowing against your cash value, but will need to repay them, with interest, to preserve the death benefit portion of the policy;

3. You can use the cash (in some cases) to pay off your premiums once the cash value reaches a certain level;
4. You can use the cash to increase the death benefit left to your loved ones after you die;
5. You can supplement another form of retirement savings, such as a 401k or IRA;
6. You can surrender the policy and withdraw all of the cash value in the policy if you no longer need life insurance. However, you should note that if you decide to surrender your coverage to the insurer and cash out early, there will be fees charged that will take away from the policy's cash value; and,
7. You could sell your life insurance policy to a third party for a cash settlement.

Although extra cash in your pocket sounds tempting, there is a lot to think about when choosing a cash value insurance policy over the standard term life insurance. First, there are different forms of cash value life insurance in which to choose. Second, cash value life insurance, compared to investing in stocks, usually have a lower rate of return. Third, cash value life insurance has higher premiums, higher fees from the insurance company, and higher commissions from agents.

There are four different types of cash value life insurance in which to choose: Whole life insurance, Variable life insurance, universal life insurance, and indexed universal life insurance. However, the next section will only discuss two popular choices that are vastly different, whole life insurance and indexed life insurance.

The way the cash value portion of your life insurance policy works depends on the type of policy you have, and deciding on which type of permanent life insurance to choose ultimately depends on how much risk you are willing to take with your cash.

Whole Life Insurance

This is the most common type of permanent life insurance because it's the most straightforward. This type of insurance guarantees a fixed rate of return on your cash value. The annual price you pay, the death benefit your beneficiaries receive, and the return you attain on the cash value component are all clear, uncomplicated, and upfront.

Whole life offers a savings component for the duration of your entire life and allows you to build your cash value at a fixed rate (determined by the insurer). This type of insurance is designed to reach the size of the death benefit when the policy matures. As for the death benefit, as long as your premiums are paid, while life insurance will provide your loved ones a death benefit after you die.

This is what makes whole life insurance such an attractive form of permanent life insurance – it offers a death benefit while still allowing you to build a cash value you can borrow against. A guaranteed death benefit plus a guaranteed cash value makes for a very attractive permanent life insurance plan.

Through your whole life insurance plan, your cash grows by earning interested at a pre-determined rate by the insurer, and your premiums remain level over the course of your life. This type of cash value insurance plan is definitely the least risky compared to other permanent life insurance options because whole life insurance offers a guaranteed cash value. Essentially, it operates similar to a standard savings account; the policy earns interest at a predetermined rate. However, whole life insurance premiums are still more expensive than other plans. The premiums are much more expensive than term life insurance and the return on investment takes a much longer period of time to accrue (sometimes 12-15 years) than if you would have invested your monies into another type of investment or life insurance option. If you are a younger investor with a limited amount of cash to use to buy insurance as well as invest for your future, whole life insurance may not be ideal for you. Instead, it may be better to get a life insurance plan that has a much cheaper premium so that you can then take those monies you are saving and invest them into a more lucrative savings plan (such as the 401(k), IRA, or HSA plans we noted earlier).

Whole life insurance makes it easy to take advantage of the cash value portion of your policy, but it does come with a price. That being said, this cash value builds over time and the policy holder can make withdraws, as needed, or borrow against the monies that act as a savings component within the policy itself. The cash value within whole life insurance earns a guaranteed minimum amount of interest and can serve as a solid investment plan.

Although you cannot deduct your whole life insurance premiums on your tax return, and they would have been a pricey deduction, there are many tax-free benefits that will be discussed below. In addition, when your beneficiaries receive the death benefit portion of this policy, they will not have to pay federal taxes on this death benefit amount. All in all, the risk on whole life insurance is low: you will have a predictable rate of return, fixed premiums, and guaranteed death benefits for your loved ones.

NOTE: You cannot increase your living and death benefits under whole life insurance unless you add a paid-up policy. This option is not available with all whole life insurance plans, so you will need to contact your specific insurance to see if this option is available. If it is, paid-up additions is essentially additional insurance that allows the policy holder to increase their living and death benefits by increasing the cash value. This could be a valuable option if you have a very large cash value in your plan but you do not need to use it on yourself while you are living. Instead, it can be used to make sure your family does not lose this additional cash value that you have built up over the years.

Paid-up additions also allow you to pay premiums using the policy's cash value due to this conversion because the cash value ends up being substantial enough to allow you to stop paying premiums out-of-pocket. The cash value of paid-up additional insurance increases over time, which is tax-deferred. Basically, a paid-up addition gives a higher guaranteed net cash value sooner than a basic whole life insurance plan. Paid-up additions earn dividends, which compound value over time. However, each premium payment, if paid with the cash value, is also deducted from the policy's death benefit.

Buying paid-up additions does not require more medical exams or underwriting, although it is very similar to buying a smaller, single-premium life insurance policy. So, if your health has gotten worse over time, you can still look into purchasing paid-up additions as an added benefit to your plan.

Indexed Universal Life Insurance

This second option gives a cash value benefit based upon the performance of a market index like the S&P 500. Therefore, the funds do not earn a fixed rate of interest similar to whole life insurance but, since the monies are not directly invested into the stock market, there is less risk with this preference. So, this is another potential option to build cash value over the long term. How does this work?

Your insurer will choose the index, calculate an interest based on the chosen index's performance, and then credits the interest to your cash value account. However, you do not lose everything if the market crashes since indexed universal life insurance guarantees a minimum interest rate to be paid even if the index produces lower returns.

That being said, this plan is also subject to a cap on the upper interest limit even if the market goes through the roof.

Below are some of the benefits of an Indexed Universal Life Insurance plan:

1. Adjustable premium payments (within certain limits) and the ability to use your cash value to pay your premiums.
2. Adjustable death benefit, which can be lowered at any time (increasing them is more complicated and may require a new medical examination).
3. The ability to withdraw funds from the cash value portion of the policy or borrow against it (subject to interest charges). These monies can be accessed at any time, regardless of your age. However, this may reduce your death benefit or cause your policy to lapse if you do not maintain a certain balance within the cash value portion of the account.

4. Tax-deferred cash accrual while preserving a death benefit for loved ones.

In the end, indexed universal life insurance is a good mixture of many different forms of permanent life insurances discussed above. It offers the potential of interest growth based on how the market performs, but also guarantees a certain amount of protection from losing all of its value if the market tanks.

Remember…while whole life insurance guarantees a fixed rate interest model that may not have a huge potential growth factor, variable life insurance grows with the market, which could offer potential highs as well as potential lows. Universal life is a good mixture of the two in that it offers fixed-rate models and variable ones to invest in if you wish. Indexed universal life is a good option if you want to allocate your cash value amounts to either a fixed or equity index account based on popular indexes like the S&P 500. These policies may be more unpredictable than universal life insurance. However, they are less risky than variable universal life policies and still may see larger growth than whole life insurance.

In the end…indexed universal life insurance may be a great option for those who desire a cash value that can grow through a solid equity index along with the protection of permanent life insurance through a guaranteed death benefit. Its flexibility and safety all wrapped up into one! That being said, you need to have an understanding of the fees and costs of this type of plan. These fees can be somewhat hidden and extremely high. For example, did you know that with these plans you may have administrative expenses deducted monthly from the cash value portion of your policy? What about a premium expense change, which could actually be deducted from the premium you pay before it is even applied to the actual case value of your plan? And, there could more than likely be upfront annual fees and commissions that are taken out of your account on the same date each year for the insurance experts that are setting up and then continuing to manage your account. Finally, you need to be aware that these plans also have what is called surrender charges – the amount of your own money you will actually forfeit if you cancel the plan early or withdraw funds. In fact, in some cases taking even a partial withdraw will permanently reduce the death benefit, which could hurt the amount of money your loved ones will receive later in life. You need to have an understanding of these front-loaded and additional fees that are built into these plans and may be confusing to investors when trying to decide the best place to invest their monies.

Although the above fees may become cumbersome, it's still worthy to note that, in this type of plan, the total amount of your cash value is credited, with interest based on any increases in an equity index. Because there is less risk than variable policies, this form of permanent insurance guarantees a minimum fixed interest rate along with a varied choice of indexes in which to choose. In addition, you can also decide what percentage you would like allocated to the fixed and indexed portions of your accounts! Basically, the value of your selected indexed is documented at the beginning of the month and then compared to the value at the end of the month. If you see an increase in your index, this interest is added to your cash value. That is, your index gains are credited back to your policy. For example:

If you see a 7% increase from beginning of September to the end of that month, this 7% is then multiplied by your cash value and the subsequent interest is then added to that cash value. Now, if the index goes down, then no interest is credited to the cash account. But, you are still protected in this plan from losing everything! Basically, your goal is to outperform the chosen market index.

This, however, could also be seen as a con since the insurance company has the ability to cap your highs and lows. But, this option is also attracted because, since there is some risk, the premiums will more than likely be lower than the whole life insurance option. In addition, your cash value can pay your insurance premiums if you build enough equity, allowing you to all but stop making out-of-pocket payments.

If you would like the security of a fixed universal life policy or whole insurance and the interest-earning potential of a variable policy, indexed universal life is a great option!

Remember...

Depending on which type of cash value life insurance policy you choose will determine what dividends you earn from your payments each month. Dividends are not guaranteed for each and every cash value life insurance policy, but when they are distributed they are according to the type of policy you have and the amount of your cash value. In addition, you may have an insurance company that pays you what's called an "annual dividend." This is usually money that is left over from what premiums you paid that year after the insurance company's expenses and claims are paid. These are also nontaxable since the IRS deems them as a return of your premium, not a traditional dividend. You can use these dividends for a variety of things, from withdrawing them as cash, to buying additional coverage, to beefing up your death benefit, or even paying your monthly premiums.

There are seven ways you can use this cash so that you ensure this money remains yours and is not unintentionally forfeited over to the insurance company:

1. Withdraw your funds: At any point during your life, you can withdraw cash from your permanent life insurance policy up to your policy's basis (i.e., the amount you have paid into the policy for your premiums). Basically, with cash value life insurance, the portion of the payments you make towards your premiums build the cash value portion of the account and forms your policy's basis. This is essentially your funds, so you are free to withdraw your own cash for emergencies, vacations, pay of bills, help pay for retirement, whatever you like.

You will need to find out if your specific policy allows for unlimited withdraws or a finite amount each calendar year, as each permanent life insurance plan is different. Also remember that your withdrawal is only tax-free if it does not exceed the amount you have already paid into the cash value portion of your policy. This is very important to be aware of, as you do not want to end up paying taxes on your withdrawals.

In addition, your death benefit will be reduced based on the amount you withdraw, so make sure your timing is right and your beneficiaries will not need the full death benefit amount at that time. That being said, if your beneficiaries are adult children, for example, who are financially stable and may not need a larger inheritance, you may want to withdraw a portion of your cash value for your own needs and still pass on a smaller inheritance. Just be aware that your cash withdrawals can take a financial toll on your death benefits or even wipe the entire amount out without you realizing it until it is too late.

Experts do not recommend making these types of partial withdrawals if you have a whole life insurance policy because the death benefit may be reduced at a greater amount than your withdrawal. That is, the death benefit for your beneficiaries ends up being reduced at a greater amount than what you actually withdrew for cash. However, making a partial withdrawal using an indexed universal life insurance policies, which has the investment option, is usually less complicated. As long as you do not withdraw more than your policy's basis – the amount you have paid for your premiums – you can make partial withdrawals tax free and they only reduce the death benefit payment by the exact amount you withdraw.

2. Take out a loan: Another option to accessing the cash portion of your permanent life insurance policy is taking out a loan from the cash value portion of your insurance plan. This process is different from making a standard withdraw because you are basically borrowing *against* your policy.

Normally, you have the ability to borrow the amount up to the cash value of your insurance policy. Because your premium payments are split each month between the cash value and death benefit, the amount you borrow can also include the portion of your paid premiums that have gone towards the cash value portion of your account and any accrued interest on those monies. Therefore, you can borrow from your cash value account, tax free, if you need a loan with low interest rates that does not have a specific date in which it needs to be paid back.

This option acts like any other traditional loan; you make an agreement on the amount you would like loaned to you and the insurance issuer will charge interest on the outstanding principal of the loan. This interest is an additional charge, usually lower than most standard interest rates, so it will need to be paid out-of-pocket or, if available, from the cash value portion of the insurance plan. If you do not pay the interest annually, it will simply be added to the amount of the loan needed to be paid back. However, interest will continue to accrue, so manage your loan wisely. Although you can keep the loan as long as you would like, note that you will continuously accrue interest on those funds.

Similar to withdrawing cash outright, your outstanding loan amount also reduces the death benefit. If the interest on the loan remains unpaid, the insurance company may deduct that amount from the cash value that remains in the permanent life insurance policy. In addition, if you die before your loan is paid off, the remaining amount will be subtracted from the death benefit your beneficiaries will receive from the policy.

In addition, don't forget that, like any other loan, the loan you take out against your permanent insurance policy accrues interest. This accruing amount could also chip away at your policy's death benefit since the loan amount, plus interest, is deducted from the death benefit allocated to your beneficiaries if you die and these amounts are paid off. So, think wisely before taking out a loan against your cash value life insurance policy. Although the low interest rates are attractive, adding a loan, plus interest, to your financial obligations may not be wise due to the negative effects it could have on your death benefit.

Finally, taking out a loan is ultimately dependent on how much cash value you have in your account. Remember that whole and indexed universal life insurance policies, although very low risk, take time to build and may not be liquid enough to borrow against right away. That being said, if you have accumulated a generous cash value within your life insurance policy then choosing to take out a loan could be very beneficial financially.

Borrowing against your cash value is the perfect choice if your insurance policy has a very high cash value or if you are looking to "re-invest" these funds at a higher rate of return than the interest you are accruing on the loan itself. The interest will be lower than your traditional bank loan and you are not obligated to pay it back in a specified amount of time. As long as you are aware that you must pay back the interest, and the loan itself, before you die, you may want to take out a loan from your permanent life insurance policy versus taking out a loan from your traditional bank.

3. Pay your policy premiums: Once you have accumulated a sufficient amount of cash value, indexed universal life insurance policies, and paid-up portions of whole life insurance policies, give you the opportunity to use your policy's cash value to pay off your insurance premiums. Once the cash value portion of your life insurance policy is to a certain amount that it can cover the payments, this cash value can also be used to pay your policy premiums in lieu of paying them out-of-pocket. This is a very advantageous feature of permanent life insurance policies versus term life insurance since permanent life insurance usually costs more than term.

Because a portion of your premium payments each month goes into building the cash value of your policy, these monies can be made available to pay off your premiums when times are financially tough. As long as you have a sufficient amount of funds in this cash value portion, you can stop paying your premiums out-of-pocket and, instead, have the cash value portion of your policy cover them.

If you decide to use this option with your accrued cash, you need to carefully monitor the cash value of your policy to make sure it does not drop too low. If you do not monitor how much cash is being used to pay for your premiums, you may end up depleting all of the cash in this portion of your life insurance policy. If you exhaust the cash value of your life insurance policy then your policy will lapse, which will terminate your life insurance coverage. Therefore, you need to make sure your cash value is not too small if you want to use it to pay off your insurance premiums. That being said, if you have a sizable amount of cash built up in your policy, and your variable or universal life insurance plans have consistent returns on investment, you can keep your life insurance and not pay premiums for years and years.

FOR EXAMPLE: If your variable or universal life insurance policy has an annual premium of $2,500 and you have $100,000 in cash value, you would only need to make 2.5% interest annually to pay off your premiums in their entirety using your cash value and not lose any money!

This option is usually not available with standard whole life insurance policies. Since the cash value of whole life insurance policies usually grow at a slower (but less risky) rate, whole life insurance policies usually do not allow policy holders to use the cash to pay premiums unless a paid-up policy is purchased. Paid-up additions to your whole life insurance plan acts like a smaller, additional insurance policy that can be used to increase the living and death benefits or to use the cash to pay off premiums. Adding this paid-up option is a valuable alternative if you have a very large cash value in your plan but you do not need to use it on yourself while you are living. Instead of withdrawing the funds or taking out a loan for yourself, you can simply use it to pay off your annual premiums and never pay them out-of-pocket again.

Paid-up additions are an advantageous option for whole life insurance holders to pay premiums using the policy's cash value because the cash value ends up being substantial enough to allow you to stop paying premiums out-of-pocket. This paid-up addition gives a higher guaranteed net cash value sooner than a basic whole life insurance plan and earn dividends, which compound value over time. However, each premium payment, if paid with the cash value, is deducted from the policy's death benefit and could end up giving you less cash value available for other purposes, such as a policy withdrawal or loan.

Nearly all indexed universal and "paid-up" whole life insurance policies allow policy holders to pay for life insurance premiums using the cash value portion of the policy, but some plans may have limitations. For example, some plans only allow you to use your accumulated cash to pay for premiums after you have the policy for a minimum of one year. Other polices require enough cash value to subsidize the policy for a minimum of 60 days in order to complete the request. That being said, if you have enough cash to stop paying your premiums out-of-pocket, you could be saving yourself thousands of dollars in expenses each year.

4. Increase your death benefit: Maybe you have accumulated a generous cash value within your permanent life insurance policy over time and simply do not need to use the funds on yourself. If this is the case, it may be a great idea to use this cash to leave an even larger death benefit to your beneficiaries.

You can use your cash to increase the death benefit simply by transferring the funds from the cash portion of your permanent life insurance policy to the death benefit portion just takes a phone call; let your insurance company know you are interested in increasing the death benefit using the cash value portion of your policy. Just make sure your insurance company will honor this request without limitations.

If you have the means, you should try to deplete as much of your cash value as possible so that those monies go towards your beneficiaries when you die, not the insurance company.

5. Supplement your retirement savings: Why not combine the investment options discussed in the "basic" option portion of this book by using the cash value you have accumulated in your permanent life insurance account to strengthen your current retirement portfolio, whether it is for your 401(k), your traditional or Roth IRA, or your HSA.

Whole life insurance, in particular, can be a very worthwhile complement to your retirement plans when you are ready to retire. Unlike term life insurance, which more than likely will run out when you are ready to retire, a whole life insurance policy will cover you until you die. In addition, the monies in whole life insurance grow tax-deferred, which can accumulate a hefty nest egg over time for your retirement years. However, if you find you do not need this policy when you are ready to retire, while not cash it out, save money on the monthly premiums, and use the cash value as retirement funds in one of your other investment options?

You can also use the cash value portion of your life insurance policy as a strategy to save money for retirement or supplement your retirement funds. For example, if the market has a bad year, which does not affect a whole life insurance policy but does affect your IRA, you can use the cash value portion of your policy instead of your retirement savings. That way, you can allow your IRA to replenish after a bad market year and, instead, make withdraws from your whole life insurance plan.

6. Surrender your permanent life insurance policy: If you find you no longer need your permanent life insurance policy, you can surrender it back to the insurance company and collect the cash value (minus any loans, unpaid premiums, and additional fees). Surrendering your permanent life insurance really just involves a simply phone call to tell your insurance agent you know longer want

to carry your insurance coverage and they will begin the cash-out process. If you are curious as to how much net cash value you would receive from a surrender it is usually listed separately on your permanent life insurance statements as the "actual" surrender value of the policy. However, you should take many life, financial, and health factors into consideration before taking this finite route to accessing your cash.

Probably the most important consideration when contemplating a full surrender is the death benefit. If you surrender your permanent life insurance policy, you will also be surrendering the death benefit portion of your policy meant for your loved ones. What does this mean? Basically, your beneficiaries will no longer receive those funds when you die.

It is important to understand that the actual net cash value will be lower than the total value you have accumulated over the years because there will be additional fees assessed. Therefore, if you decide to surrender your permanent life insurance policy, this option will reduce the cash value you ultimately receive. It is recommended that you hold on to your policy for a minimum of ten to 15 years to make sure the net cash value is closer to the total accumulated cash value you have built over time. That being said, you can surrender the value of your policy after at least three years of holding that policy and accumulating some cash value. This may not be a smart move, however, in that the surrender fees could eat up the smaller cash value you accumulated over this shorter period of time. In addition, if you surrender the policy during what is known as the "surrender period," which is anywhere between the first two to three years of ownership, you may not receive any cash value or be subject to even more additional, larger fees. You should talk to your insurance agent about the potential surrender fees that could be assessed depending on how long you have owned your permanent life insurance policy.

You should also be aware that the cash you ultimately receiving after you surrender your insurance will be subject to income tax. Any money you receive from the surrender that is over the "cash basis" (how much you originally paid into the policy) can be taxed accordingly.

Probably the most important thing to note, however, is if you surrender your life insurance you and your loved ones are no longer protected if you die. A surrender essentially means you are giving up your insurance policy. Now, you do receive the cash value, less any fees, and there is no interest or repayment that you would have if you took out a loan against the policy. But, surrendering your policy means you will no longer have life insurance, your beneficiaries will no longer have a death benefit, and because of this you should have an alternative plan in place for further protection against uncertainties.

7. Sell your permanent life insurance policy for a settlement: The final option to attaining the cash value of your permanent life insurance policy is to opt for what's called a "life settlement. You are still giving up your life insurance policy, similar to an all-out surrender, but in this case you are selling your policy to a third party for essentially a cash sale. This could be a very advantageous option if the premiums for your policy are too high and unaffordable, your beneficiaries are financially secure on their own, or you no longer have beneficiaries to obtain your death benefit after you die.

If you are interested in going this route, the first question you will need to ask yourself is whether or not you can even sell your life insurance policy for a cash settlement. If you can find a company willing to purchase your life insurance policy for more than the cash value but less than the death benefit, this is a profitable option. The main benefit of selling permanent life insurance versus term life insurance is that a company will more than likely purchase your permanent life insurance at any stage of your life. With term life insurance, however, a company will usually only buy this policy for cash if you are likely to die during the policy term due to age or sickness.

If you choose to sell your permanent life insurance policy for cash, you will be required to pay both income and capital gains taxes on this settlement. In addition, if you have trouble selling your life insurance on your own and decide to hire a business broker to facilitate the transaction, he or she will also be paid a portion from the settlement. That being said, selling your life insurance is usually more lucrative than surrendering your policy to the insurance company. Finding a buyer to purchase your permanent life insurance policy is not easy and could take several weeks or even months. Therefore, you may need assistance with a sales professional.

What happens once the policy is sold and you are paid? The life insurance settlement company will take over your premium payments and will become the new beneficiary of your policy.

COMPLEX OPTION 2: 1031 Exchanges

Not many people have even heard of 1031 Exchanges, but this is another more complex investment option that could be used to grow and earn money. But, if you invest in real estate, this could be a great way to refocus your monies on new properties while saving money on the frustrating capital gains taxes normally associated with a real estate sale.

Let's say you own investment property and are thinking about selling it and buying another property. This is where the 1031 Exchange can be used as an investment vehicle to help you save money. This type of procedure allows you, the investment property owner, to sell it and buy another property while deferring capital gains tax.

All of these benefits are in the IRC Section 1031. Under this section, a properly structured 1031 Exchange (and there is a lot that goes into properly structuring your exchange, as discussed below!) allows an investor to sell a property (the relinquished property), to reinvest the proceeds in a new property (the replacement property) and to defer all capital gain taxes. IRC Section 1031 (a)(1) requires the investor to only exchange property of like kind and only exchange property that is considered to be a business, not personal investment (to be explained below).

First, we will review what a 1031 Exchange is and then delve deeper into how you can use this as an investment vehicle to grow and earn money.

What is a 1031 Exchange?

Basically, a 1031 Exchange is a tax-deferment strategy that allows an investor to sell an investment property and "defer" the capital gains taxes on the sale. How is this done? They make sure they purchase another property called a "like-kind property" with the profit gained by the sale of the first property.

Please note that this is not for personal use; instead, this option is only for investment (or business) properties. Therefore, you cannot complete a 1031 Exchange on your home. For example: If you move from Pennsylvania to California, you could not swap the residents in order to save on taxes even if they are the exact same type of residence. But, if you purchase a property strictly for investment purposes – that is, you are renting the property out for investment – and then you wish to release that property a few years later but do not want to pay capital gains tax, this is where a 1031 exchange will come into play. Maybe your real estate investment is in a high tax bracket and the capital gains you would pay on the sale would horribly undercut any profit you could make from the sale. Instead, why not exchange it for a like property, save on taxes, and continue profiting from a new investment venture.

Personal property such as franchise licenses for businesses, aircraft, and other equipment do not qualify nor do corporate stock or partnership interests (although interests as tenants in common do).

As long as you meet the requirements of a 1031 Exchange, you will not have to pay capital gains taxes on your sale. This essentially allows your investment to grow tax deferred.

Think of this scenario. You own a rental home and you've paid off the mortgage and now receive a pretty steady rental income from the tenants. Then you find out there is an even more profitable investment opportunity out there! Instead of holding onto your rental property, you exchange that property for something that meets your financial and even lifestyle needs even better! This new property has better returns on investment and less headaches that creep into your everyday life. That is the value of a 1031 Exchange.

Selling a property can be very intimidating, similar to selling a home. So, many times investors will hold onto an investment property for way too much longer than they should. What if you have a rental home and you are having trouble maintaining the property, fixing the plumbing, paying the taxes, etc.? What if the property value becomes static or you can no longer maximize on the depreciation of said property? Holding onto this property could have dire consequences on your finances and well-being if you can no longer maintain the property for renters. Instead, maybe you can find a like kind rental that, for the same investment, already has someone doing the day-to-day maintenance while you can reap the same amount or even higher amount of profits. Maybe you can exchange for a property that has greater depreciation or is in a much more desirable market for your changing lifestyle. Because a 1031 exchange allows the equity from one real estate investment to roll over right into another one, and giving the bonus of deferring the capital gains taxes, it could be the perfect solution to get out of a cumbersome investment while building new wealth in a new one over time.

The IRS has not put any limit on 1031 Exchanges – you could essentially complete as many as you'd like. In fact, you can even roll over the gain from one investment into another as long as they meet the like-kind property requirements. However, there are special rules that every investor must understand fully when exchanging depreciable property using a 1031 exchange. Be sure you are not activating what is called a depreciation recapture, which could actually be taxed as ordinary income. To avoid this depreciation recapture, you will need to make sure you are basically swapping one building for another building, not a building with improved land for a building without improved land because the depreciation claimed on the first building will need to be recaptured as ordinary income.

What does "like-kind" mean?

Before we discuss the basics of this complex investment option, we should define what "like-kind" even means because it is a very broad phrase. For example, there may be an instance where you exchange an apartment building that houses tenants for a strip mall, or a business for raw land. You could also exchange a single family home that is used as a rental property for a restaurant space, or a vacation rental for a commercial office building. This is because, the term like-kind can constitute properties that are basically in the same nature or character. For example an apartment building would more than likely be considered like-kind for another apartment building. But, you could also possibly exchange that same apartment building for a real estate home if they are in the same nature or character, even if they are different in grade or quality.

Basically, you can exchange nearly any type of real estate property as long as it's not *personal property* (to be discussed in further detail below).

There are two terms you should understand before going further:

Relinquished property: This is your original investment property that you are selling.

Replacement property: This is the property you are purchasing from the sale of your relinquished property in your exchange.

NOTE: The replacement property sale price must be equal or greater value of the relinquished property or else you'll pay capital gains tax on the difference, as discussed below. Also discussed will be important timing issues: you must identify a replacement property within 45 days and then conclude the exchange within 180 days. There are also three important rules that any investor looking to deal with 1031 exchanges must be aware:

- a three-property rule: The most common rule in a 1031 exchange, which states that you can identify one, two, or even three properties and acquire one, two, or all three regardless of each property's fair market value. Just like the 45 day aspect above, the fair market value must also be identified within 45 days and the investor should trade a property that is equal or greater in value from the relinquished property being sold.

- 200% rule: If more than three properties are identified, then the investor may choose to use the 200% rule. This means the cumulative value of the identified properties does not exceed 200% of the relinquished property being sold. Again, the fair market value of the identified properties must be identified within 45 days because if the fair market value of even just one property changes and its value increases after this 45 magic number, the investor will be violating this 200% rule.

- 95% rule: This final rule allows an investor to identify as many properties as he or she would like as long as the acquired properties are valued at 95% of their total or more. For this rule, the fair market value can be determined up to the day of closing or by day 180 of this exchange period, whichever one comes first.

It is also important to understand that your exchange can include more than two properties. For example, you may want to exchange one relinquished property for multiple replacement properties (or vice versa). As long as the like-kind stipulation holds in which the replacement does not cost less than the relinquished property or properties, you can find your qualified intermediary and begin your 1031 exchange process!

As the above examples illustrate, you can literally swap one or more properties in a 1031 Exchange, in which there are two or more like-kind properties and are traded between the owners. However, this is easier said than done! As an investor, you need to realize that many 1031 exchanges will be delayed, and you will need to find a competent middleman to hold onto your cash after you sell your relinquished property before you use this same cash to essentially buy the replacement party. This is how you are using the three-party exchange swap – although you are buying a new property with the monies gained from the sale, you will not need to pay the capital gains tax because this middleman is holding the cash for you while you are finalizing your 1031 exchange.

This "middleman" noted above is also known as a qualified intermediary. Under section 1031, any proceeds from the sale in a 1031 Exchange must be transferred to a qualified intermediary, not the seller of the property. This qualified intermediary is a person or business that agrees to facilitate the 1031 Exchange by holding the funds from the purchaser and then will transfer the money to the seller of the replacement property.

Remember that the values must either be equal or the value of the replacement property must be less than the relinquished property.

So, if you can exchange one property for another property of similar value, this could be a very lucrative investment strategy in order to make money on your sale, attain a new property, and not have to pay capital gains taxes. As long as the purchase price and the new loan amount are either the same or higher on the replacement property, you can use investment option to your advantage. That is, you cannot receive a "boot" and take the tax-free advantages. A "boot" is essentially a gain in the exchange – you sell your relinquished property for more than the replacement property. If you have this difference, it is called a "boot" and you will have to pay capital gains on that "boot" portion. For example:

If you sell your relinquished property for $2 million and want to purchase a replacement property under a 1031 Exchange that is worth $1.5 million, you would need to pay the normal capital gains tax on the $500,000 "boot."

NOTE: No matter which type of 1031 Exchange you complete, you must also consider what is left on your own mortgage and any other debt you may have within your relinquished property. For example, if you had a mortgage of $2 million on your relinquished property but the mortgage on the new property is only $1,800,000, this also qualifies as a "boot" and you will need to pay taxes on this $200,000 gain.

Another stipulation to a 1031 Exchange is that the name that appears on the title of the property being sold must be the same name as on the tax return and title holder that is purchasing the new property. One exception would be if a single member liability company is selling it, since that is considered a pass-through to the member. So, the single member liability company (i.e., John Doe, LLC) may sell the property and John Doe can purchase the property in his own name since he is the sole member of the LLC.

In conclusion, tax-deferred exchanges can give investors a valuable opportunity to defer capital gains taxes on the sale of their property while increasing a return on investment in the new property from the "swap" of a 1031 exchange. In order to realize the full potential of the benefits in a 1031 exchange, it is imperative that you work with experts who have the right knowledge of the Section 1031 code. This includes having a full understanding of what "like-kind" means, understanding the function of the "middle man," and making sure you meet all of the timing rules and other rules that are so essential to this type of real estate investment. If you do all of this properly, you could see significant portfolio growth and an increased return on your investment through this lucrative 1031 exchange process.

Four Types of 1031 Exchanges

There are typically four different types of 1031 Exchanges that will be discussed here:

1. Delayed
2. Simultaneous
3. Reverse
4. Construction/Improvement

1. Delayed Exchange: This is the most common type of 1031 Exchange because it gives an investor time to find an in-kind property. A delayed exchange is when an investor sells his or her property first (i.e., the "relinquished property") and then acquires the replacement property. Basically, the purchase of the exchange is "delayed" after the original sale of the first property. The selling investor has a maximum of 45 days in which he or she can find the replacement property and 180 days to complete the sale. For example:

You have a rental property that is very high-maintenance and costing too much upkeep each month. You decide to sell that property and then later purchase a "like-kind property" with that profit that has much lower maintenance each month. Now, you've saved money because you don't have to pay capital gains on the first sale, and you continue to save money because you have much lower maintenance on this new property.

Here's how your delayed exchange would work:

1. Set the sale date and complete the sale of your relinquished property
2. Your "qualified intermediary" (the middleman) accepts the proceeds from that sale
3. Within 45 days of that sale date, you identify your replacement property
4. Your "qualified intermediary" transfers the proceeds from the sale to the seller of the replacement property
5. Within 180 days of that sale date, you complete the purchase of your replacement property.

2. <u>Simultaneous Exchange:</u> If two properties close simultaneously, that is on the same day, they could save capital gains taxes through a 1031 Exchange. This may be done through a standard "swap" between two parties or when the exchange is completed by a qualified intermediary. As long as both properties close on the same day, the sale would qualify for 1031 Exchange. Both sales must occur on the same day in order to save the capital gains taxes. For example:

You are interested in moving from one area in which you have an investment to another geographic location, but don't want to pay those pesky capital gains taxes on your sale. You can find a "like-kind property" in that new location and make the exchange on the same day to save on your capital gains taxes.

3. Reverse Exchange: This type of 1031 Exchange occurs when an investor acquires a replacement property, but then sells their relinquished property at a later date. However, this type of exchange must be paid in all cash and it may be difficult to get a bank loan for this type of exchange. Similar to the Delayed Exchange, this sale must be completed within 180 days to attain the tax benefits. For example:

You unexpectedly find an investment opportunity that you cannot pass up! But, this is before you have had time to even put your relinquished investment property on the market. You purchase the replacement property first, pay cash, and then subsequently list and sell your relinquished property. This would be the timing of your reverse 1031 Exchange:

1. You purchase the replacement property and the property is held by the qualified intermediary (aka., the exchange accommodation titleholder).
2. Within 45 days, you identify the property to sell.

3. Within 180 days you complete the sale and the exchange accommodation titleholder transfer the property to you.

4. <u>Construction/Improvement Exchange:</u> This type of exchange allows taxpayers to make improvements on a replacement property using the tax-deferred dollars saved from the exchange. All of this tax-deferred equity must be spent on the improvements within 180 days, the investor must receive the property identified within 45 days, and this replacement property must be of equal or greater value when it is deeded back to the taxpayer. For example:

You use tax-deferred dollars you saved on your relinquished property to improvement the building of your replacement property. These monies are used to renovate the outside of the building, the plumbing, and other improvements and construction. All of these improvements and construction must be completed by the time the transaction is complete. *Any improvements made after the exchange is completed will not qualify as part of the exchange!!*

There are numerous expenses and fees that can be paid with exchange funds, from qualified intermediary (middle-man) fees, to any broker's commissions that may be required, to other professional fees that come with a sale: filing attorney, tax adviser fees, finder or escrow feels, and even repair and maintenance costs.

Remember that this is still essentially a sale – you are selling a real estate property and acquiring a new one. Just because you are not paying capital gains tax does not mean there are still complications to the sale that will more than likely require a business broker, attorney, tax adviser, and numerous filings and other out-of-pocket costs.

Completing a 1031 Exchange can be a complicated process and needs to be fully reviewed in order to make sure it is the best bang for the buck. On one hand, holding on to your investment property for too long could be a mistake, but rushing to purchasing a new replacement property under the 1031 Exchange rules may not be the right choice either if it is a bad deal.

That being said, if you find a replacement property that has a better rate of return, if you are a real estate owner looking to no longer manage your own property and find one that is managed for you, or if you simply want to consolidate several properties into one, completing a 1031 Exchange could be perfect for you.

So, to wrap up this complicated process in a not so complicated way:

1. You can complete a 1031 Exchange if you find a like-kind investment opportunity for a replacement sale that is titled in the same manner as your relinquished property.

2. You identify this replacement property within 45 days and purchase the property within 180 days of closing the relinquished property.

3. The replacement property is of equal or greater value than your replacement property and is purchased using the proceeds from your replacement property.

4. Your sale is purchased through a qualified intermediary.

COMPLEX OPTION 3: Investing in Qualified Opportunity Zones

Maybe a 1031 Exchange seems too complicated of a process or you cannot find the perfect like-kind investment opportunity in your area and don't wish to move. Another investment option that could help you defer or reduce your capital gains tax could be to invest in what is called a "Qualified Opportunity Zone."

The Opportunity Zone program was created within the 2017 Tax Cuts and Job Act to improve economically distressed communities through private investors instead of through taxpayer dollars. It was a somewhat hidden way to help some of the nation's most economically-distressed communities by incentivizing the investors who put up the funds. These private investors are rewarded through capital gains tax incentives that are available through this program after they invest in a qualified opportunity zone.

This type of investment is literally a "feel good" investment, since more than 50 million Americans are living in distressed regions. They are losing jobs and may be living in violent or addiction-prone areas, making these areas literal poverty traps. When you invest in these types of areas, you are not only investing in the future of the area itself; you are investing in the future of those individuals living within those areas.

As noted by those numbers above, you as an investor could save on capital gains taxes by investing in these opportunity zones, while also helping the more than 52 million Americans living in these distressed areas.

What is a qualified opportunity zone? The IRS has determined that an Opportunity Zone is an economically-distressed area that meets certain low-income requirements. That way, new investments into those areas are given preferential tax treatment to help the investor and those living in these distressed, low income areas. How does it work? Localities are nominated by the state and then certified by the Secretary of the U.S. Treasury in order to then become an Opportunity Zone and be able to begin benefiting from future investments. There are two new Internal Revenue Code (IRC) sections that outline the Opportunity Zone program: IRC sections

1400z-1 governs the Opportunity Zones and 1400z-2 governs the Opportunity funds.

In the simplest of terms, they are composed of economically distressed communities that have been determined to qualify for the Opportunity Zone program. The criteria for this determination was outlined in the 2017 Tax Cuts and Jobs Act, and it has been found that up to 25% of low-income areas in the country that can meet the income qualifications of this program can be designated as Opportunity Zones. Nearly 9,000 Opportunity Zones have been qualified in the United States and in United States territories, such as Puerto Rico, and once a low-income neighborhood is designated as an Opportunity Zone, it can retain this designation for ten years.

As discussed above, these Qualified Opportunity Zones were established in the 2017 Tax Cuts and Jobs Act in order to provide some tax incentives for those wishing to invest in these economically distressed areas. As of June 14, 2018, the Treasury Department has certified zones in all 50 states. Actually, the entire area of Puerto Rico is considered an Opportunity Zone! There are approximately 8,700 Opportunity Zones nationwide, and a complete list can be found here:
https://www.cdfifund.gov/pages/opportunity-zones.aspx

Each state was given the opportunity to essentially nominate communities to qualify as an Opportunity Zone as long as the poverty rate in the area is at least 20% and the median family income is not more than 80% of the statewide median family income, among other more complex qualifications for the chance to be designated as an Opportunity Zone.

Like mentioned above, these investment opportunities are basically "feel good" investments for those who have the funds to put into Opportunity Zones. In fact, the reason behind the creation of these Opportunity Zones was to give incentives for economic development and create jobs in these economically distressed areas by providing tax benefits to investors. So, they can also be a valuable investment tool if used wisely. And, you do not need to live or work in the Opportunity Zone you are interested in investing to take advantage of these tax benefits.

For example…if you sold stock for a gain and during the 180-day period beginning on the date of the sale you invest that gain into a Qualified Opportunity Fund, you can defer paying any tax on that gain.

How Does This Investment Program Work?

Just like a 1031 Exchange, 180 is the magic number for investing in Qualified Opportunity Zones. You, the taxpayer, have 180 days from the date of the sale or exchange of your chosen property to invest the capital gain into a Qualified Opportunity Zone Fund. This is basically an investment vehicle that is set up specifically for investing in eligible property within a Qualified Opportunity Zone. This fund will then invest these monies into the Qualified Opportunity Zone Property.

It is important to remember the whole reason why Opportunity Zones were created before investing monies into them. Essentially, they were designed to take low-income, distressed areas and incentivize economic development into those areas. This is done by simply providing tax benefits to investors; they can defer tax on any prior gains invested into a Qualified Opportunity Zone fund. A taxpayer may also elect to defer the tax on some or all of his or her capital gains if, during the magic 180 day period beginning at the date of sale or exchange, they invest in a Qualified Opportunity Fund. Any taxable gain invested in this Qualified Opportunity Zone will not be recognized until December 31, 2026. In addition, if this investor holds onto the investment in this Qualified Opportunity Zone fund for at least ten years, the investor is then eligible for an increase in the basis of this Qualified Opportunity Zone fund that would be equal to its fair market value on the date the Qualified Opportunity Zone fund is either sold or exchanged. Truly a win-win!

If you do not want to hold onto a Qualified Opportunity Zone for a full ten years, there are other step-up options to still defer your capital gains. For example, there are 10% and 15% options to pay absolutely no tax on capital gains. If you defer capital gains through a Qualified Opportunity Zone Fund investment, you will receive a 10% step-up in tax basis after five years. If you keep this opportunity for an additional two years, you can then receive another 5% step-up.

NOTE: In order to take advantage of the 15% step-up in tax basis, you MUST invest by December 31, 2019! This is become the tax will then be triggered at the end of 2026, the date noted above. That is, the taxpayer will have held onto the investment for a full seven years, therefore qualifying for the 15% increase in tax basis. It is all about the December 31, 2026 date noted above!

Now, what if there is a loss in the value of a Qualified Opportunity Zone Fund? Yes, a loss could happen, but the taxpayer is still entitled for the increase in basis if they held onto the investment for the five or seven years noted above. When the fund reaches the mandatory deferred gain recognition date on December 31, 2026, if there is a loss the investor's recognized gain will end up being the lesser of the original deferred gain (or the fair market value of the fund interest) decreased by the taxpayer's adjusted basis in the fund. This complicated process could better be explained by an example:

An investor holds onto a Qualified Opportunity Zone Fund for seven years in order to gain the 15% step-up in tax basis. However, the Opportunity Zone Property is sold at a loss. If the investor realizes $8 million from the Qualified Opportunity Zone Fund, and the taxpayer did hold the investment for the full seven years, the investor will still receive the 15% increase in the basis, or $1,500,000. Therefore, the gain realized would end up being $6,500,000.

Basically, this program allows you to defer paying capital gains taxes if you sell appreciated investments and then reinvest that money from the sale into an Opportunity Zone Fund. And, there are no capital gains on any appreciation if the investment is kept in this Opportunity Zone Fund for at least ten years.

Because this is essentially an investment, the value of investing in an Opportunity Zone Fund may increase or decrease in value over the holding period. In order to receive your capital gain tax incentives, you must invest in a Qualified Opportunity Zone through an Opportunity Fund. There are three types of investments that would be considered a "Qualified Opportunity Zone property":

1. Any investment vehicle that is organized as an organization or partnership interest that operates in a Qualified Opportunity Zone.
2. Stock ownership in businesses that manage nearly all of their operations in the Qualified Opportunity Zone.
3. Other properties, such as real estate, that are also located in the Qualified Opportunity Zone. Opportunity funds for real estate would count towards either the construction of new

buildings or the improvement of existing, unused buildings. The latter is a great opportunity for improvement, as many of these areas having vacant buildings just sitting in areas doing nothing for the individuals living within the zones.

So, what do you get from your investment? By investing any one of the following above options into an Opportunity Zone Fund, you will receive considerable capital gains incentives on your sale, immediately, and then over the long term while your monies are invested into the program. This is because when you would normally sell an appreciated asset (like real estate or stock options), there is a capital gain involved that is taxed by the IRS. However, if you take those monies and reinvest them into an Opportunity Fund, you are given the ability to defer paying that capital gains tax. Essentially, you are reducing your tax liability on that gain you made from the original divesting of the real estate or stock. And the savings don't stop there! You can potentially receive tax-free treatment on the future appreciation earned through the fund if it stays there for at least at decade.

But, don't forget that magic 180 number…you must invest your gains into a Qualified Opportunity Fund within 180 days in order to qualify for any positive tax treatment under the Opportunity Fund program. For example:

Let's say Anthony sold a business for a $12 million capital gain in June of 2018. Anthony then identifies three properties in two Qualified Opportunity Zones that also have the same purchase price as his capital gains. If Anthony invests his $12 million into a Qualified Opportunity Fund and holds onto this fund until the December 31, 2026 date noted above, he will save more than $100,000 in taxes!!

To conclude this last complex investment opportunity, investing in a Qualified Opportunity Zone can help you save on capital gains taxes and help a community in need. Through your tax-free investment, you are assisting in the development and renovation of low-income communities across the United States.

The Treasury Department and the Internal Revenue service are still reviewing the details on investing in Qualified Opportunity Zones, and any investor should note any changes in these opportunities going forward before investing in this "feel good" opportunity. That being said, when you put your money to work in a Qualified Opportunity Zone, you can defer and reduce your capital gains tax (or even eliminate them!), and help a community that is in dire need of funds to help those community members live a better life. The bottom line is, if you are facing considerable tax payments due to capital gains, investing these monies into a Qualified Opportunity Zone Fund could be a lucrative investment option.

Wrap Up:

There are many basic options in which you can invest your money now for a healthy retirement in the future. This book compared the differences between 401(k)'s and IRA's and noted how they can both be very beneficial to an investor who would like an easy way to invest money now with little complications or effort. Investing in a Health Savings Account can also be a lucrative option if you have a high-deductible insurance plan and the opportunity to pay for your health care needs out of pocket so that your money can be saved for the long haul.

Your home is also a wonderful investment vehicle! Whether it is outright selling your home or renting it through Web sites like Airbnb and VRBO, you can definitely use your home as an investment vehicle to save for the future. Finally, investing in mutual bonds can also be a simple way to save money for the future without having to have a strong understanding of the stock market.

If you are interested in making even more money for your future with some more complicated options, why not purchase a cash value life insurance policy? Not only will you be saving money for your future, you will also be saving a lucrative death benefit for your loved ones after you are gone. While you are living, however, why not invest in real estate opportunities such as a 1031 Exchange or helping a low-income, distressed area through a Qualified

Opportunity Zone investment. Either way, you are building your own investment funds for your own future.

No matter which option you choose to invest your monies, whether basic or complicated, it is always imperative to discuss any option with a qualified professional about your income, your retirement needs, and where your money will give you the best return on investment for your future.

BONUS: A Detailed Explanation of Cash Value Life Insurance

An Introduction to Cash Value Life Insurance

There are numerous ways to invest wisely to earn money and attain tax-free monetary growth. But, one method many individuals don't know about is using cash value life insurance policies to do just this – earn money and attain tax-free growth while investing income wisely.

Everyone knows that life insurance is a way to protect your loved ones financially if you die. But, many people don't realize that cash value life insurance acts as an investment, with a savings component built into your life insurance. This cash component gains value, tax-deferred with interest, as the years go by and can be borrowed against or used as collateral, similar to a loan, when you need some extra cash.

How does this work? Cash value life insurance policies provide monetary coverage while you are living, as well as a death benefit that will go to your loved ones after you die. Each month you pay your premiums similar to term life insurance. However, with a cash value life insurance policy, a portion of your premiums are paid into an investment-type account (i.e., the cash value), while the remainder goes towards death benefits for your beneficiaries. The portion that goes into the investment-type account grows through accruing interest over time (depending on which type of cash value life insurance plan you choose). This cash value is essentially "liquid" and can become a valuable source of income when times are tough or in the case of an emergency.

Although extra cash in your pocket sounds tempting, there is a lot to think about when choosing a cash value insurance policy over the standard term life insurance. First, there are different forms of cash value life insurance from which to choose. Second, cash value life insurance usually has a lower rate of return compared to investing in stocks. Third, cash value life insurance has higher premiums, higher fees from the insurance company, and higher commissions from agents.

That being said, cash value insurance policies are not just for the rich and America's "elite" one percent. If researched, chosen, and used correctly, a cash value life insurance plan can become a lucrative savings account that can be used to withdraw funds, attain a loan, or even pay off your very own insurance premiums. All of these benefits are available with cash value life insurance, in addition to growing a death benefit that will protect your loved ones after you die. Isn't that the whole point of life insurance? To protect your beneficiaries after you die?

Yes, the main function of life insurance is to ensure your family's financial well-being after you are no longer there to provide for them financially. Just think of all the bills you pay every day – mortgage, food, entertainment, college education...the list can go on and on. If you aren't there to pay these bills, your life insurance plan is there to replace your income. But, what if you could also benefit from your life insurance plan while you were living? That is what cash value life insurance offers you.

You can withdraw funds or take out a loan in case of an emergency; you can build another nest egg to be used towards your retirement; you can pay off your premiums with the cash invested instead of paying them out of pocket. You can even boost the death benefit for your loved ones with this extra cash. All in all, a cash value life insurance plan allows you to use these funds while you are living, while also protecting those you love after you die. And, all of this is done tax free!

This article will discuss the following in detail:

1. Cash value life insurance (also called permanent life insurance) versus term life insurance.
2. The different types of cash value life insurance:
    a. Whole life insurance;
    b. Variable life insurance;
    c. universal life insurance, and
    d. indexed universal life insurance.
3. How cash value life insurance makes money.
4. How you can get and use your cash:
    a. Withdraw funds;
    b. Take out a loan;
    c. Pay off your premiums;
    d. Boost your death benefit;
    e. Build your retirement;
    f. Surrender the life insurance policy;
    g. Sell your life insurance to a third party.

Most people think life insurance is only a way to make provisions and protect your loved ones after your death. But, what if you could invest in life insurance that also builds a cash value to be used at a later date while you're still alive? That's exactly the benefit of cash value life insurance. A cash value life insurance plan will protect your loved ones after you die through a death benefit that pays out when the policyholder dies, but will also serve as a liquid financial savings account while you're living. This is because your premiums are split between the death benefit and a cash value (along with any fees and overheads the insurance company charges to provide the coverage). This cash value operates as a tax-sheltered investment plan and earns interest on your premium payments. You can use these earnings while you are alive to withdraw as cash, attain a loan, or even pay your monthly premiums.

IMPORTANT NOTE: Because the cash value portion of your life insurance policy is separate from your death benefit, your beneficiaries would not receive this cash benefit if you die before it is used. That is, they will receive the death benefit promised, but not the cash value earnings in the investment portion of the policy. Instead, this cash portion is returned to the insurance company since it is basically the liquid amount you would have received if you would have cancelled your coverage. So, you need to make sure you use this money while you are alive so the cash value isn't surrendered to your insurance policy if you pass away!

What is Cash Value Insurance versus Term Life Insurance?

Term life insurance is the other option one can choose to protect their loved ones. If you choose term life insurance, you are basically insuring yourself for a specific number of years and, if you die during those chosen years, the insurance company pays your loved ones. However, if you outlive the term, the policy simply ends and you don't receive any cash. On the other hand, cash value life insurance does have a death benefit for your loved ones similar to term life insurance, but also gives you cash-on-hand while you are living.

As long as you, the policyholder, make your regular premium payments to keep your policy active, your beneficiaries will receive what's called a "death benefit" – an agreed-upon amount of money – after you die. But, cash value life insurance also has an investment element that can earn interest, build over time, and be available for withdrawal at a later date. Essentially, cash value is a "living" benefit of life insurance; the monies don't sit stagnant only to be used after you die. Instead, you can take cash out when you are living in lieu of waiting until after your death, in which case the cash goes to your beneficiaries.

How does this work? Your premium payments are split between funding the death benefit portion and funding the cash value of your plan. Over time, the cash value component – essentially, your savings or investment component – grows while the death benefit shrinks. In addition, if you, the policy holder, die after the cash value of the policy is fully realized, the entire amount paid to your beneficiaries ultimately comes from the cash value side, not the death benefit side.

Cash value life insurance is a form of permanent life insurance; that is, it is a policy that provides lifetime coverage and flexibility to cancel your policy, attain the cash value of your policy, or withdraw monies for emergencies. While term life insurance guarantees a death benefit to your beneficiaries at a specific time – your death – permanent life insurance provides coverage and cash value while you are living. As long as the premiums are paid, cash value life insurance provides coverage for your entire life. Term life insurance does not include a cash value, which is why they are usually more affordable than permanent life insurance options.

Cash value life insurance policies usually have higher premiums that term life insurance due to the added lifetime flexibility. That being said, a cash value policy earns interest and defers taxes on these accumulated earnings. The only circumstance in which you could get cash back from a term life insurance policy is if you have a return of premium rider – an add-on policy that returns the premiums you have paid if you outlive the term of the policy. Otherwise, if you decide to just have term life insurance coverage with the insurer, you will not receive anything in return because term life insurance policies do not have a cash value.

So, while your term life insurance provides temporary coverage over a certain period of time – 10, 20, 30, 50 years – it provides no additional cash value. You cannot borrow against a term life policy or cash it in for money if you need it. This is what makes term life insurance so much more affordable since the premiums are usually lower than permanent life insurance. Although cash value life insurance is pricier, it offers an additional savings component.

Another benefit of cash value life insurance is the stability of the insurance itself. You are going to be insured under the plan in spite of how your health may change over time. If your health begins to decline and you have term life insurance, you may need to purchase another term (also called "re-upping" your coverage), which may come with higher premiums when you are at your most vulnerable. This is not the case with cash value life insurance; with this type of policy, you are covered even if your health changes over time. Although you are paying higher premiums with this plan, these premiums remain a flat rate no matter what health issues you may encounter as you get older.

As the policyholder of a cash value policy, you are able to use the cash value of your policy for numerous purposes, whether you need a loan to be paid back at a later date, cash on hand, or even money to help pay your premiums. How does this work?

What Types of Permanent Life Insurance Have Cash Value?

The way the cash value portion of your life insurance policy works depends on the type of policy you have, and there are four types of permanent life insurance policies that have a cash value: whole life, variable life, universal life, and indexed universal life insurance. Deciding which type of permanent life insurance to choose ultimately depends on how much risk you are willing to take with your cash.

Whole Life Insurance – This is the most common type of permanent life insurance because it's the most straightforward. This type of insurance guarantees a fixed rate of return on your cash value. The annual price you pay, the death benefit your beneficiaries receive, and the return you attain on the cash value component are all clear, uncomplicated, and upfront.

Whole life offers a savings component for the duration of your entire life and allows you to build your cash value at a fixed rate (determined by the insurer). This type of insurance is designed to reach the size of the death benefit when the policy matures. As for the death benefit, as long as your premiums are paid, while life insurance will provide your loved ones a death benefit after you die.

This is what makes whole life insurance such an attractive form of permanent life insurance – it offers a death benefit while still allowing you to build a cash value you can borrow against. A guaranteed death benefit plus a guaranteed cash value makes for a very attractive permanent life insurance plan.

Through your whole life insurance plan, your cash grows by earning interest at a rate pre-determined by the insurer, and your premiums remain level over the course of your life. This type of cash value insurance plan is definitely the least risky compared to other permanent life insurance options because whole life insurance offers a guaranteed cash value. Essentially, it operates similar to a standard savings account; the policy earns interest at a predetermined rate.

Whole life insurance makes it easy to take advantage of the cash value portion of your policy. This cash value builds over time and the policy holder can make withdraws, as needed, or borrow against the monies that act as a savings component within the policy itself. The cash value within whole life insurance earns a guaranteed minimum amount of interest and can serve as a solid investment plan.

Although you cannot deduct your whole life insurance premiums on your tax return, there are many tax-free benefits that will be discussed below. In addition, when your beneficiaries receive the death benefit portion of this policy, they will not have to pay federal taxes on this death benefit amount. All in all, the risk on whole life insurance is low: you will have a predictable rate of return, fixed premiums, and guaranteed death benefit for your loved ones.

NOTE: You cannot increase your living and death benefits under whole life insurance unless you add a paid-up policy. This option is not available with all whole life insurance plans, so you will need to contact your specific insurance provider to see if this option is available. If it is, paid-up additions is essentially additional insurance that allows the policy holder to increase their living and death benefits by increasing the cash value. This could be a valuable option if you have a very large cash value in your plan but you do not need to use it on yourself while you are living. Instead, it can be used to make sure your family does not lose this additional cash value that you have built up over the years.

Paid-up additions also allow you to pay premiums using the policy's cash value due to this conversion because the cash value ends up being substantial enough to allow you to stop paying premiums out-of-pocket. The cash value of paid-up additional insurance increases over time, which is tax-deferred. Basically, a paid-up addition gives a higher guaranteed net cash value sooner than a basic whole life insurance plan. Paid-up additions earn dividends, which compound over time. However, each premium payment, if paid with the cash value, is also deducted from the policy's death benefit.

Buying paid-up additions does not require more medical exams or underwriting, although it is very similar to buying a smaller, single-premium life insurance policy. So, if your health has gotten worse over time, you can still look into purchasing paid-up additions as an added benefit to your plan.

Variable life insurance – This type of insurance also covers you for the duration of your life and has a guaranteed death benefit. However, variable life insurance does not hold the guaranteed cash value seen with whole life insurance. Instead, your money is invested in various "sub-accounts," which are a pool of in-house investor funds offered by the insurer. This is how your cash grows (or shrinks) over time.

With this type of plan, your cash value will grow similar to a traditional investment plan; that is, it grows at the interest rate of a predetermined index specifically chosen by the life insurance company. Your cash value is invested in specifically-chosen aggregated portfolios, similar to mutual funds, but this means your cash is less insulated from market fluctuations. While whole life insurance works similar to a standard savings account, variable life insurance works similar to a standard investment account. Although the premiums for this plan are also fixed, some variable life insurance accounts may offer "adjustable" premiums, which allow you to change, modify, or adjust your premium and death benefit options as you continue to invest the cash value into the sub-accounts offered by the life insurance company.

This type of plan holds more risk than the standard whole life insurance option, including the risk of possessing a more expensive insurance plan that could end up with little or no cash value depending on the market, because your cash growth is tied to a stock index (such as the Standard & Poor's 500). So, you could either gain the greatest returns on your money if your stocks, bonds or mutual funds do well, or you could lose your cash value if your investments tank. Is there reward with this investment risk? Yes…variable life insurance gives you the opportunity to invest in sub-accounts that may offer higher rates of return.

That being said, this type of plan has additional rewards that can outweigh any investment risk. For example with a variable life insurance plan your premiums are adjustable. What does that mean? You have the option to skip a premium payment or even stop paying your premiums all together if the cash value of your policy can cover those costs (similar to universal life insurance, discussed below). This option is very helpful if you have an emergency and need to skip a premium payment or two during those more difficult months. In addition, if you transfer funds between investments, you can do this tax-free, in addition to your ability to withdraw funds or take a loan out against the cash value when times are tough. Just make note of what these withdraws may do to your death benefit.

Finally, if your insurance needs change as you age, you can either increase or decrease your coverage under this plan, whether it is on your death benefit or on the policy's cash value.

Flexibility is key to this permanent insurance plan. If you enjoy reviewing different investment options and can take the time to better understand where you should invest your funds, variable life insurance allows for these flexible possibilities. The main aspect to understand is, like any other type of investment option, there is always the possibility of loss when playing the market, which would reduce your policy's cash value.

Universal life insurance – Another option that covers you for the duration of your life and offers a guaranteed life benefit is universal life insurance. This type of policy is less risky than variable life insurance since the guaranteed cash value is protected from investment risk since the cash grows at a fixed interest rate. However, these monies could also be depleted to pay for premiums. In addition, these premiums are not level; instead, they vary and are subject to federal tax laws.

How does universal life insurance work? Similar to the other options, when you pay your premiums each month a portion of each payment builds up your cash value while the other portion goes towards the death benefit. However, a universal life insurance policy also offers flexibility with premiums; this type of insurance has the option to adjust your premiums and death benefit, similar to the variable life insurance option. If you hold a universal life insurance policy, you have the option to either lower your premiums or even stop paying them as long as the cash value of your policy can cover the monthly costs. This is a very advantageous option when times are tough. You just always need to make sure your cash value can cover your premium costs.

Along with this benefit, you will continue to earn a cash value through interest, and you can withdraw money or take out a loan against it similar to whole and variable life insurance. As long as you take note that the amount you withdraw or borrow many reduce the policy's death benefit in certain cases, similar to variable life insurance, this option is a good mixture of the benefits of both whole and variable life insurance.

How is the risk with this plan different from whole and variable life insurance? The cash value portion of a universal life insurance policy earns interest similar to the current money market rates. Although this means the interest earned may go down if the market goes down, some universal plans do offer a minimum performance guarantee with these types of policies.

Although universal and variable life insurance are very similar, there are significant differences between universal life insurance and whole life insurance that must be understood in order to make the best decision of permanent life insurance. Both offer lifelong protection and a cash value as long as premiums are paid, but:

1. Adjustable versus fixed premiums – Universal life insurance policies allow for the ability to adjust your premium amounts, while whole life insurance only offers fixed premiums and death benefits.
2. Adjustable versus fixed death benefit – Similar to the premiums, universal life insurance policies also allow for the ability to adjust your death benefit amount, while this benefit remains fixed if using the whole life insurance option.
3. Interest on cash value differences – Universal life insurance interest is in line with the current money market rates, which could mean hefty rewards or unfortunate losses. Whole life insurance offers a guaranteed rate of return, which lowers the risk when earning interest. However, this also does not allow for the benefit of higher interest earnings when the market is doing well.

In short, universal life insurance plans allow you to vary your premiums and your death benefit coverage amount. They also offer varying levels of risk depending on the market – there is a strong potential for gains for your cash value if you choose a universal life insurance plan.

Indexed Universal Life Insurance – This final option gives a cash value benefit based upon the performance of a market index like the S&P 500. Therefore, the funds do not earn a fixed rate of interest similar to whole life insurance but, since the monies are not directly invested into the stock market, there is less risk with this plan. So, this is another potential option to build cash value over the long term. How does this work?

Your insurer will choose the index, calculate an interest based on the chosen index's performance, and then credits the interest to your cash value account. However, you do not lose everything if the market crashes since indexed universal life insurance guarantees a minimum interest rate to be paid even if the index produces lower returns.

That being said, this plan is also subject to a cap on the upper interest limit even if the market goes through the roof.

There are other similarities between this type of plan and the others discussed:
5. Adjustable premium payments (within certain limits) and the ability to use your cash value to pay your premiums.
6. Adjustable death benefit, which can be lowered at any time (increasing them is more complicated and may require a new medical examination).
7. The ability to withdraw funds from the cash value portion of the policy or borrow against it (subject to interest charges).

These monies can be accessed at any time, regardless of your age. However, this may reduce your death benefit or cause your policy to lapse if you do not maintain a certain balance within the cash value portion of the account.
8. Tax-deferred cash accrual while preserving a death benefit for loved ones.

In the end, indexed universal life insurance is a good mixture of all three forms of permanent life insurances discussed above. It offers the potential of interest growth based on how the market performs, but also guarantees a certain amount of protection from losing all of its value if the market tanks.

Remember…while whole life insurance guarantees a fixed rate interest model that may not have a huge potential growth factor, variable life insurance grows with the market, which could offer potential highs as well as potential lows. Universal life is a good mixture of the two in that it offers fixed-rate and variable rate models to invest in if you wish. Indexed universal life is a good option if you want to allocate your cash value amounts to either a fixed or equity index account based on popular indexes like the S&P 500. These policies may be more unpredictable than universal life insurance. However, they are less risky than variable universal life policies and still may see larger growth than whole life insurance.

In the end...indexed universal life insurance may be a great option for those who desire a cash value that can grow through a solid equity index along with the protection of permanent life insurance through a guaranteed death benefit. Its flexibility and safety all wrapped up into one!

Basically, the total amount of your cash value is credited, with interest based on any increases in an equity index. Because there is less risk than variable policies, this form of permanent insurance guarantees a minimum fixed interest rate along with a varied choice of indexes in which to choose. In addition, you can also decide what percentage you would like allocated to the fixed and indexed portions of your accounts! Basically, the value of your selected index is documented at the beginning of the month and then compared to the value at the end of the month. If you see an increase in your index, this interest is added to your cash value. That is, your index gains are credited back to your policy.

For example:

If you see a 7% increase from the beginning of September to the end of September, this 7% is then multiplied by your cash value and the subsequent interest is then added to that cash value. Now, if the index goes down, then no interest is credited to the cash account. But, you are still protected in this plan from losing everything! Basically, your goal is to outperform the chosen market index.

This, however, could also be seen as a con since the insurance company has the ability to cap your highs and lows. But, this option is also attractive because, since there is some risk, the premiums will more than likely be lower than the whole life insurance option. In addition, your cash value can pay your insurance premiums if you build enough equity, allowing you to all but stop making out-of-pocket payments.

If you would like the security of a fixed universal life policy or whole insurance and the interest-earning potential of a variable policy, indexed universal life is a great option!

Remember...

Depending on which type of cash value life insurance policy you choose will determine what dividends you earn from your payments each month. Dividends are not guaranteed for each and every cash value life insurance policy, but when they are distributed they are according to the type of policy you have and the amount of your cash value. In addition, you may have an insurance company that pays you what's called an "annual dividend." This is usually money that is left over from the premiums you paid that year after the insurance company's expenses and claims are paid. These are also nontaxable since the IRS deems them as a return of your premium, not a traditional dividend. You can use these dividends for a variety of things, from withdrawing them as cash, to buying additional coverage, to beefing up your death benefit, or even paying your monthly premiums.

How Can My Cash Value Life Insurance Make Me Money?

As discussed above, cash value life insurance is a form of permanent life insurance that offers two features:

3. A death benefit – the amount of money that is paid out to your beneficiaries when you die.
4. Cash value – an investment-like feature that accrues cash to be used in a variety of ways while you are alive.

Each month, a portion of your premiums are paid into the investment portion of your policy, while the remainder goes into the death benefit for your loved ones protection. The benefits? Tax-free earnings and cash on hand for a variety of options, from withdrawals and loans to paying premiums and saving for retirement:

Tax-free earnings: Probably the best advantage of cash value life insurance is the tax advantage. Similar to other investment options, the cash value of your life insurance policy and the earnings it accrues are tax-free. You can continue to keep these funds tax-free as long as you only withdraw an amount that does not go over what you have paid in premiums. Therefore, it is recommended to not withdraw more than this amount, as you will have to pay taxes on the difference between what you have already paid in premiums and the amount of cash you are taking out of your policy. The basic rule of thumb is to only make a tax-free withdraw up to the amount you have already paid into the cash-value portion of your insurance policy. If your withdraw exceeds that amount, it will then become taxable income.

<u>Cash on hand:</u> The reason individuals decide to purchase permanent life insurance is because of the cash value. This is the main benefit of cash value life insurance – you have cash on hand if needed while you are living. This is because the cash value element of your policy is basically an investment plan. Therefore, you can do many things with this cash that is similar to a traditional investment tool. The important thing to note, however, is the cash portion of your permanent life insurance plan is a "use it or lose it" scenario. This cash will not be available to your beneficiaries after you die unless you allocate it to the death benefit portion of your plan before your passing.

FOR EXAMPLE: Let's say you hold a policy that has a $50,000 death benefit and you have accumulated $5,000 in cash value. Upon your death, your insurance will pay the full death benefit of $50,000 to your beneficiaries. However, the $5,000 you saved in the cash value portion of your policy will ultimately go back to the insurance provider. So technically, the real liability cost to the insurance company is $45,000 since they retain your $5,000 in cash. After you die, your beneficiaries receive the death benefit, but any remaining cash value will be returned to the insurance company. So, you will need to spend this cash value while you are living!

There are seven ways you can use this cash so that you ensure this money remains yours and not the insurance company's:

8. You can simply withdraw the funds, but if the money is not repaid these withdraws will reduce the policy's death benefit;
9. You can take out a loan by borrowing against your cash value, but will need to repay it, with interest, to preserve the death benefit portion of the policy;
10. You can use the cash (in some cases) to pay off your premiums once the cash value reaches a certain level;
11. You can use the cash to increase the death benefit left to your loved ones after you die;
12. You can supplement another form of retirement savings, such as a 401k or IRA;
13. You can surrender the policy and withdraw all of the cash value in the policy if you no longer need life insurance. However, you should note that if you decide to surrender your coverage to the insurer and cash out early, there will be fees charged that will take away from the policy's cash value; and,
14. You could sell your life insurance policy to a third party for a cash settlement.

1. Withdraw your funds: At any point during your life, you can withdraw cash from your permanent life insurance policy up to your policy's basis (i.e., the amount you have paid into the policy for your premiums). Basically, with cash value life insurance, the portion of the payments you make towards your premiums build the cash value portion of the account and forms your policy's basis. This is essentially your money – your savings so to speak – so you are free to withdraw your own cash for emergencies, vacations, payment of bills, to help fund retirement, whatever you like. Maybe you are low on funds one month or have a large purchase you would like to make and do not have the cash on hand. As long as you do not exceed this basis, these withdrawals will not be taxed. However, if you withdraw more than your basis, these monies will be taxed at your current income tax rate.

You will need to find out if your specific policy allows for unlimited withdrawals or a finite amount each calendar year, as each permanent life insurance plan is different. Also remember that your withdrawal is only tax-free if it does not exceed the amount you have already paid into the cash value portion of your policy. This is very important to be aware of, as you do not want to end up paying taxes on your withdrawals.

NOTE: Although withdrawing funds gives you access to cash that can be used for anything you need, it is important to note that your death benefit will also be reduced based on the amount you withdraw, so make sure your timing is right (that is, your beneficiaries will not need the full death benefit amount at that time!). That being said, if your beneficiaries are adult children, for example, who are financially stable and may not need a larger inheritance, you may want to withdraw a portion of your cash value for your own needs and still pass on a smaller inheritance. Just be aware that your cash withdrawals can take a financial toll on your death benefit or even wipe the entire amount out without you realizing it until it is too late.

These "partial withdrawals" are handled differently depending on what type of permanent life insurance plan you choose. For example, experts do not recommend making partial withdrawals if you have a whole life insurance policy because the death benefit may be reduced at a greater amount than your withdrawal. That is, the death benefit for your beneficiaries ends up being reduced by a greater amount than what you actually withdrew in cash. However, making a partial withdrawal using variable and universal life insurance policies, which have the investment option, are usually less complicated. As noted above, as long as you do not withdraw more than your policy's basis – the amount you have paid for your premiums – you can make partial withdrawals tax free and they only reduce the death benefit payment by the exact amount you withdraw.

2. Take out a loan: Another option for accessing the cash portion of your permanent life insurance policy is taking out a loan from the cash value portion of your insurance plan. Taking out a loan is a very common way to access funds from a cash value life insurance policy. This process is different from making a standard withdraw because you are basically borrowing *against* your policy. Normally, you have the ability to borrow the amount up to the cash value of your insurance policy. Because your premium payments are split each month between the cash value and death benefit, the amount you borrow can also include the portion of your paid premiums that have gone towards the cash value portion of your account and any accrued interest on those monies. Therefore, you can borrow from your cash value account, tax free, if you need a loan with low interest rates that does not have a specific date by which it needs to be paid back.

This option acts like any other traditional loan; you make an agreement on the amount you would like loaned to you and the insurance issuer will charge interest on the outstanding principal of the loan. This interest is an additional charge, usually lower than most standard interest rates, so it will need to be paid out-of-pocket or, if available, from the cash value portion of the insurance plan. If you do not pay the interest annually, it will simply be added to the amount of the loan needed to be paid back. However, interest will continue to accrue, so manage your loan wisely. Remember, life insurance companies are like any other business – their main goal is to make money. And, since they cannot make money off of you if you take your money out of your plan (yes, the insurance company, like a standard bank, will use your money that is sitting in your plan to cover overheads, invest, and pay other people's claims) they will instead charge you interest to make up those differences. Although you can keep the loan as long as you would like, note that you will continuously accrue interest on those funds.

However, you do not need a credit check like traditional loans, so a loan from your cash value life insurance will not appear on your credit report like other loans would. In addition, there are not any underwriting requirements since the insurer basically holds the funds to cover the loan already and there is no time limit on the loan – you can keep it as long as you need.

The process for applying for this type of loan is also much easier than a standard loan from a bank. These monies can be used for anything, from improving your home, to buying a car, to paying off financial obligations.

Similar to withdrawing cash outright, your outstanding loan amount also reduces the death benefit. If the interest on the loan remains unpaid, the insurance company may deduct that amount from the cash value that remains in the permanent life insurance policy.

NOTE: Although there is no time limit on how long you can keep your loan, if you die before your loan is paid off, the remaining amount owed will be subtracted from the death benefit your beneficiaries will receive from the policy. For example, if you take out a loan and then are in a plane crash (morbid, but it happens), and the loan is more than the death benefit, your family will not receive a penny from your cash value life insurance policy. Instead, the death benefit will be used to pay off your loan. This is simply because the loan is connected to your death benefit as well as the cash value portion of your insurance policy plan. Therefore, before you decide to take a loan out against your cash value life insurance policy, ask yourself one question: *if I day the day after I take out a loan against my life insurance, will there still be enough money in the death benefit portion of the plan to take care of my family? Isn't this the reason you took out life insurance in the first place? To take care of your loved ones in the event of your passing?*

So, the question remains, when is a suitable time to borrow against your cash value life insurance policy? If you need a loan but a conventional loan from your bank is not an option, either because of high interest rates or a low credit score, then taking out a loan against your permanent life insurance policy is a great option. If you have the opportunity to get a conventional loan from your bank, however, with a lower interest rate, this is often the better choice in the long run for both you and your beneficiaries.

In addition, don't forget that, like any other loan, the loan you take out against your permanent insurance policy accrues interest. This accruing amount could also chip away at your policy's death benefit since the loan amount, plus interest, is deducted from the death benefit allocated to your beneficiaries if you die and these amounts are paid off. So, think wisely before taking out a loan against your cash value life insurance policy. Although the low interest rates are attractive, adding a loan, plus interest, to your financial obligations may not be wise due to the negative effects it could have on your death benefit. In addition, most loans must have income taxes paid on the amounts, and if the size of your loan exceeds the value of your policy (possibly because of unpaid interest) your policy will lapse and your coverage will be dropped. This is why you need to monitor the loan, especially because there is no deadline on which it needs to be paid back. The interest on the cash you borrow for your loan will accrue continuously and possibly chip away at the death benefit portion allocated for your loved ones.

In the end, borrowing against your cash value life insurance could be an advantageous financial choice, but ultimately depends on one's current financial and health situation. What are your current financial and health circumstances? What plans do you have for this loan and ultimately paying it back, plus interest? You need to weigh the advantages and disadvantages to borrowing against your cash value, as well as your current life situations and circumstances, also compare this to taking out a loan with your bank.

Finally, taking out a loan is ultimately dependent on how much cash value you have in your account. Remember that whole and universal life insurance policies, although very low risk, take time to build and may not be liquid enough to borrow against right away. That being said, if you have accumulated a generous cash value within your life insurance policy, then choosing to take out a loan could be very beneficial financially. Borrowing against your cash value is the perfect choice if your insurance policy has a very high cash value or if you are looking to "re-invest" these funds at a higher rate of return than the interest you are accruing on the loan itself. The interest will be lower than your traditional bank loan and you are not obligated to pay it back in a specified amount of time. As long as you are aware that you must pay back the loan ,as well as the interest before you die, you may want to take out a loan from your permanent life insurance policy versus taking out a loan from your traditional bank.

In the end, just remember that the whole point of life insurance, even a cash value life insurance plan, is to provide financial stability to your loved ones after you pass away. If you borrow too much against your policy, you risk not having anything left for your beneficiaries if you die unexpectedly. That being said, you can use your loan for anything – even to pay your premiums and keep your insurance stable if times are tough financially. Or, you can even pay off your premiums using the cash value portion of your permanent life insurance policy.

3. Pay your policy premiums: Once you have accumulated a sufficient amount of cash value, variable and universal life insurance policies (and paid-up portions of whole life insurance policies) give you the opportunity to use your policy's cash value to pay your insurance premiums. Once the cash value portion of your life insurance policy reaches a certain amount where it can cover the payments, this cash value can also be used to pay your policy premiums in lieu of paying them out-of-pocket. This is a very advantageous feature of permanent life insurance policies versus term life insurance since permanent life insurance usually costs more than term.

With a term life insurance plan, the money you pay to cover your insurance premiums does not have any return on investment. The insurance company keeps these monies and you cannot claim these funds during your lifetime. However, with cash value life insurance, a portion of your payments goes into building the cash value of your policy. Therefore, these monies can be made available to pay your premiums when times are financially tough. As long as you have a sufficient amount in this cash value portion, you can stop paying your premiums out-of-pocket and, instead, have the cash value portion of your policy cover them.

This option of how to attain your cash can be very attractive – you are short on cash so you decide to stop paying your insurance premiums and, instead, earmark the cash value portion of your policy to cover them. But like anything else when it comes to using the cash value portion of your life insurance policy, there are aspects of which you must be aware.

First, you need to carefully monitor the cash value of your policy to make sure it does not drop too low. If you do not monitor how much cash is being used to pay for your premiums, you may end up depleting all of the cash in this portion of your life insurance policy. If you exhaust the cash value of your life insurance policy then your policy will lapse, which will terminate your life insurance coverage. Therefore, you need to make sure your cash value is not too small if you want to use it to pay off your insurance premiums. That being said, if you have a sizable amount of cash built up in your policy, and your variable or universal life insurance plans have consistent returns on investment, you can keep your life insurance and not pay premiums for years and years.

FOR EXAMPLE: If your variable or universal life insurance policy has an annual premium of $2,500 and you have $100,000 in cash value, you would only need to make 2.5% interest annually to pay off your premiums in their entirety using your cash value and not lose any money!

Since the cash value of whole life insurance policies usually grows at a slower (but less risky) rate, whole life insurance policies usually do not allow policy holders to use the cash to pay premiums unless a paid-up policy is purchased. As discussed earlier, paid-up additions to your whole life insurance plan acts like a smaller, additional insurance policy that can be used to increase the living and death benefits or to use the cash to pay off premiums. Adding this paid-up option is a valuable alternative if you have a very large cash value in your plan but you do not need to use it on yourself while you are living. Instead of withdrawing the funds or taking out a loan for yourself, you can simply use it to pay your annual premiums and never pay them out-of-pocket again.

Paid-up additions are an advantageous option for whole life insurance holders to pay premiums using the policy's cash value because the cash value ends up being substantial enough to allow you to stop paying premiums out-of-pocket. This paid-up addition gives a higher guaranteed net cash value sooner than a basic whole life insurance plan and earns dividends, which compound in value over time.

However, each premium payment, if paid with the cash value, is deducted from the policy's death benefit and could end up giving you less cash value available for other purposes, such as a policy withdrawal or loan.

Nearly all variable, universal, and "paid-up" whole life insurance policies allow policy holders to pay for life insurance premiums using the cash value portion of the policy, but some plans may have limitations. For example, some plans only allow you to use your accumulated cash to pay for premiums after you have had the policy for a minimum of one year. Other polices require enough cash value to subsidize the policy for a minimum of 60 days in order to complete the request. That being said, if you have enough cash to stop paying your premiums out-of-pocket, you could be saving yourself thousands of dollars in expenses each year.

<u>4. Increase your death benefit:</u> Maybe you have accumulated a generous cash value within your permanent life insurance policy over time and simply do not need to use the funds on yourself. If this is the case, it may be a great idea to use this cash to leave an even larger death benefit to your beneficiaries. But, how is this done?

Usually, transferring the funds from the cash portion of your permanent life insurance policy to the death benefit portion just takes a phone call; let your insurance company know you are interested in increasing the death benefit using the cash value portion of your policy. Just make sure your insurance company will honor this request without limitations.
If you have the means, you should try to deplete as much of your cash value as possible so that those monies go to your beneficiaries when you die, not the insurance company.

FOR EXAMPLE: If you have a variable life insurance policy with a $500,000 death benefit and $100,000 in cash value, and you know you do not need to spend that $100,000 on yourself, you should transfer the entire cash amount to increase the death benefit to $600,000. That way, the extra $100,000 in cash – which is *your* money – will go to your loved ones and not the life insurance company if you die unexpectedly.

<u>5. Supplement your retirement savings:</u> Nearly all of us have some form of retirement plan to live on once we are no longer working, whether it is a 401(k) from our current job or a traditional or Roth individual retirement account. However, if you have accumulated a hefty cash value in your permanent life insurance account, these funds can be used to strengthen your current retirement portfolio.

Whole life insurance, in particular, can be a very worthwhile complement to your retirement plan when you are ready to retire. Unlike term life insurance, which more than likely will run out when you are ready to retire, a whole life insurance policy will cover you until you die. In addition, the monies in whole life insurance grow tax-deferred, which can accumulate a hefty nest egg over time for your retirement years. However, if you find you do not need this policy when you are ready to retire, why not cash it out, save money on the monthly premiums, and use the cash value as retirement funds?

You can also use the cash value portion of your life insurance policy as a strategy to save money for retirement or supplement your retirement fund. For example, if the market has a bad year, which does not affect a whole life insurance policy but does affect your IRA, you can use the cash value portion of your policy instead of your retirement savings. That way, you can allow your IRA to replenish after a bad market year and, instead, make withdraws from your whole life insurance plan.

6. <u>Surrender your permanent life insurance policy:</u> If you find you no longer need your permanent life insurance policy, you can surrender it back to the insurance company and collect the cash value (minus any loans, unpaid premiums, and additional fees). Surrendering your permanent life insurance isn't complicated, as you simply tell your insurance agent you no longer want to carry your insurance coverage and they will begin the cash-out process. If you are curious as to how much net cash value you would receive from a surrender it is usually listed separately on your permanent life insurance statements as the "actual" surrender value of the policy. However, you should take many life, financial, and health factors into consideration before taking this irreversible route to accessing your cash.

Probably the most important consideration when contemplating a full surrender is the death benefit. If you surrender your permanent life insurance policy, you will also be surrendering the death benefit portion of your policy meant for your loved ones. What does this mean? Basically, your beneficiaries will no longer receive those funds when you die.

NOTE: The actual net cash value will be lower than the total value you have accumulated over the years because there will be additional fees assessed. Therefore, if you decide to surrender your permanent life insurance policy, this option will reduce the cash value you ultimately receive. So, you should hold on to your policy for a minimum of ten to 15 years to make sure the net cash value is closer to the total accumulated cash value you have built over time. That being said, you can technically surrender the value of your policy after a minimum three years of holding that policy and accumulating cash value. This may not be a smart move, however, in that the surrender fees could eat up the smaller cash value you accumulated over this shorter period of time. In addition, if you surrender the policy during what is known as the "surrender period," which is anywhere between the first two to three years of ownership, you may not receive any cash value or be subject to even more additional, larger fees. You should talk to your insurance agent about the potential surrender fees that could be assessed depending on how long you have owned your permanent life insurance policy.

You should also be aware that the cash you ultimately receive after you surrender your insurance will be subject to income tax. Any money you receive from the surrender that is over the "cash basis" (how much you originally paid into the policy) will be taxed accordingly.

Probably the most important thing to note, however, is if you surrender your life insurance you and your loved ones are no longer protected if you die. A surrender essentially means you are giving up your insurance policy. Now, you do receive the cash value, less any fees, and there is no interest or repayment like you would have if you took out a loan against the policy. But, surrendering your policy means you will no longer have life insurance, your beneficiaries will no longer have a death benefit, and because of this you should have an alternative plan in place for further protection against uncertainties.

If you decide to go down the route of surrendering your permanent life insurance policy, you should first talk to your life insurance agent or your financial adviser. You could also consider selling your life insurance plan to a third party.

7. *Sell your permanent life insurance policy for a settlement:* The final option for obtaining the cash value of your permanent life insurance policy is to opt for what's called a "life settlement. You are still giving up your life insurance policy, similar to an all-out surrender, but in this case you are selling your policy to a third party for essentially a cash sale. This could be a very advantageous option if the premiums for your policy are too high and

unaffordable, your beneficiaries are financially secure on their own, or you no longer have beneficiaries to obtain your death benefit after you die.

If you are interested in going this route, the first question you will need to ask yourself is whether or not you can even sell your life insurance policy for a cash settlement. If you can find a company willing to purchase your life insurance policy for more than the cash value but less than the death benefit, this is a profitable option. The main benefit of selling permanent life insurance versus term life insurance is that a company will more than likely purchase your permanent life insurance at any stage of your life. With term life insurance, however, a company will usually only buy this policy for cash if you are likely to die during the policy term due to age or sickness.

NOTE: If you choose to sell your permanent life insurance policy for cash, you will be required to pay both income and capital gains taxes on the settlement. In addition, if you have trouble selling your life insurance on your own and decide to hire a business broker to facilitate the transaction, he or she will also be paid a portion from the settlement. That being said, selling your life insurance is usually more lucrative than surrendering your policy to the insurance company. Finding a buyer to purchase your permanent life insurance policy is not easy and could take several weeks or even months. Therefore, you may need assistance from a sales professional.

What happens once the policy is sold and you are paid? The life insurance settlement company will take over your premium payments and will become the new beneficiary of your policy.

The Bottom Line...
Is Cash Value Life Insurance Right for You?

As you can see, there are different forms of cash value life insurance and many different points to consider, making this form of permanent life insurance much more complicated than a simple term life insurance policy. You should discuss all of your options, your current financial and health situation, your beneficiaries, and any other issues with a life insurance professional and your financial adviser to see if cash value life insurance is right for your personal situation.

If you simply want to protect your family after you are gone and want simplicity with fixed premium payments that are inexpensive, term life insurance may be a better option for you. For example, young families that may not be able to afford the higher premium payments that come with permanent life insurance, but still want protection for their young children, may be better-served by a basic term life insurance plan. In addition, families that are still building their retirement accounts – 401(k)s, IRAs, etc. – may be better served allocating their funds into those accounts rather than a cash value life insurance policy. Cash value life insurance policies are more expensive than term life insurance, but there are still many circumstances in which cash value life insurances policies are the way to go:

- High-income earners with, somewhat, multifaceted finances who are more liquid and can allocate funds into the cash value portion and the death benefit portion of permanent life insurance.
- Middle-class families who would like to build cash up slowly through a whole life insurance plan, which is less expensive than the investment-type plans, while also building the death benefit for their beneficiaries.
- Individuals who may have contributed up to the limits of their retirement accounts and would like another avenue for savings that comes with interest gains based on the market, such as variable and universal life insurance policies.
- Families who are simply looking for, and can afford, another savings vehicle to be used later to cover debts, pay off insurance premiums, or complete a large purchase in the future.
- Those who have long-term savings goals may find the tax-deferred savings aspect of a cash value life insurance plan

very profitable. In particular, a permanent policy plan like variable or universal life insurance would be very beneficial in this type of long-term situation.

The above bullets are just a few circumstances in which cash value life insurance could benefit an individual or family. Although these types of permanent life insurance policies are more complicated than term, they can be very useful options for saving money while you are living and protecting your loved ones when you are gone. Just remember that the premiums involved with a cash value life insurance plan can be expensive, so it is imperative that you have an understanding of how and when you should use the cash portion of your funds.

Whether you want to withdraw cash to pay off debt, take out a loan for that new pool or car, or pay off your insurance premiums, permanent life insurance can be a very beneficial, tax-free, way to save money.

One final note: if you have now decided to purchase a permanent life insurance plan, make sure you figure out what you are looking for before you decide between whole, variable, universal, or indexed life insurance. The cash you grow is tax-deferred, but will compound much differently based on the plan you choose. If you are older and do not have the applicable amount of time to grow your cash value – which may take several years – you may want to talk to a professional before looking into cash value life insurance.

Made in the USA
Columbia, SC
16 January 2021